Comptroller of the Currency
Administrator of National Banks

An Examiner's Guide to

Problem Bank Identification,

Rehabilitation,

and Resolution

PROBLEM BANK IDENTIFICATION, REHABILITATION AND RESOLUTION

A Guide for Examiners

January 2001

Table of Contents

Introduction

The OCC is committed to bank supervision policies and procedures that support prompt detection and mitigation of problems before they affect a bank's viability. In the event a bank's condition is so severe that it is no longer viable, the OCC will collaborate with the Federal Deposit Insurance Corporation (FDIC) and other regulators to achieve a timely final resolution in a manner that will result in the least cost to the deposit insurance fund. This booklet provides guidance toward those objectives and is intended primarily as a reference tool for OCC field examiners.

One of the most challenging and important aspects of a bank examiner's job is knowing how to read and react, in a balanced and effective way, to symptoms of problems that may not yet be obvious to bank management and directors. The point at which an examiner identifies potential problems and recognizes the possible effect on a bank's condition is critical. This is sometimes the last point in time when an examiner may make a difference, through effective communications and moral suasion, in whether the bank rights itself or becomes a problem bank requiring enforcement action. Examiners will recognize and sometimes refer to such banks as "borderline" or "dirty 2's," referring to the imminence of a CAMELS downgrade to a "3" if conditions worsen.

It is not unusual for officers and directors of banks such as these to overlook or deny the potential seriousness of problem symptoms at this stage. Indeed, it sometimes boils down to who is more confident in their assessment of the fundamental issues - the banker or the examiner, and whether the examiner has prioritized his/her findings by order of significance. [1] This makes it all the more important for the examiner to be well prepared with documented findings and supporting opinions from the supervisory office and, when necessary, from district and headquarters risk experts.

It also is not unusual for examiners, after full discussion of the issues, to give bankers the benefit of the doubt when problem symptoms are first detected. This is most frequently the case when it is a close call, and the banker has dealt successfully with problems in the past. This normally is the correct course, because it leaves remedial action where it most appropriately belongs - with bank officers and directors - rather than with the regulators, whose government-directed solutions can be more burdensome and expensive. Examiners must be careful, however, not to extend this self-correction phase longer than is reasonably necessary for the bank to fix the problem. Unwarranted extensions of time or failures by examiners to monitor and enforce interim progress can result in recoverable situations deteriorating into serious, intractable problems. They also violate the intent of the "Safety and Soundness," "Prompt Corrective

---

[1] Failure to prioritize findings, or presenting significant issues as part of a "laundry-list," can obscure the importance of serious issues, lead to misunderstandings, and delay corrective action, especially in banks not accustomed to significant criticism.

Action," "Early Resolution," and "Least Cost Resolution" sections of the Federal Deposit Insurance Corporation Improvement Act (FDICIA).[2]

Obviously, this can be a fragile phase in the banker-examiner relationship that requires a skilled, tactful, and balanced approach to accomplish supervisory objectives without alienating the banker. The risk of damaging an otherwise harmonious relationship with a banker, however, is never an acceptable reason for an examiner to avoid or defer bringing legitimate, significant concerns to the attention of bank management and directors. Early confrontation and action usually reduces the ultimate cost of correcting problems considerably.

If, despite these efforts, the bank does not improve or continues to deteriorate, the examiner will be faced with a second critical point in dealing with a problem bank. The examiner must evaluate the situation and determine whether rehabilitation continues to be a realistic possibility for the bank or if the point has been reached where additional measures are not likely to prevent continued deterioration. In that event, eventual receivership or other resolution of the bank becomes increasingly more likely, and supervision of the bank includes planning for resolution.

This guide deals with both early detection and rehabilitation of problem banks and advanced supervision and resolution when conditions are more serious.

- **Problem Bank Identification**
  Discusses red flags and other identifiers examiners should recognize in the early detection of problems. It also focuses on OCC early warning tools, documentation of supervisory risks, and effective communication techniques in conveying problems.

- **Rehabilitation of Problem Banks**
  Provides guidance on supervision strategies designed to rehabilitate problem institutions. This includes an overview of the corrective action process, focusing on the requirements of the Prompt Corrective Action provisions of FDICIA and other OCC enforcement powers. It highlights the relevant considerations in determining the appropriate supervisory response to asset, capital, and liquidity problems.

- **Resolution Management**
  Addresses the terminal stages of supervision of institutions with a high likelihood of failure, including the need to identify such banks promptly and consider appropriate action. These materials highlight coordination within the OCC and with other regulators and supervisory issues related to the line review process, grounds for receivership and early resolution, capital call meeting, bid process, and the bank closing process.

- **Accounting Issues in Problem Banks**
  Provides a focused discussion of accounting issues routinely encountered in the supervision of problem banks. This section discusses: asset valuation, including FAS 125; sale and leasebacks; loss carryforwards and deferred tax assets; accounting rules for write-downs,

---

[2] FDICIA enacted in 1991 generally limited examiner discretion and prescribed certain actions relating to problem banks.

OREO, troubled debt restructures and timing of loss recognition; and disclosures in financial reports, including reporting errors and window dressing.

- **Problems in Large and Multi-Charter Banking Companies**
  Provides a discussion of the unique features associated with supervision of problematic large banks and multibank companies, including systemic risk determination and cross-guaranties.

- **Problems in Federal Branches and Agencies**
  Provides a discussion of the unique features associated with supervision of federal branches and agencies, including how risk in the foreign banking organization or the home country can affect the federal branch or agency.

- **OCC Appeals Process**
  Provides a summary of the OCC's appeal process, discussing considerations unique to appeals made by banks experiencing significant safety and soundness problems.

This guide is intended to complement, but not replace appropriate consultation with the supervisory office and other divisions as appropriate, including Special Supervision and Fraud, Capital Policy, Bank Accounting, Credit Risk, Treasury and Market Risk, and Law.

Problem Bank Identification

The banking system weathered a crisis in the 1980s and early 1990s. More than 1,600 banks failed or received FDIC financial assistance during this period. The cause of failures or near failures cannot be described in absolute terms; however, excessive risk-taking without effective risk management contributed in some manner to most of them.

The 1980s and early 1990s was also a period of major legislative and regulatory change affecting the financial services industry. More statutes and regulations pertaining to banks were put in place during this period than at any other time since the Great Depression. Many of those changes, especially those found in the Federal Deposit Insurance Corporation Improvement Act of 1991 (FDICIA), altered the framework for problem bank supervision.

FDICIA was designed to ensure timely identification and least cost resolution of problem banks. As discussed later in this guide, these FDICIA changes limit examiner discretion in certain instances, but clearly do not eliminate the critical need for examiner judgment. In exercising this judgment, examiners are expected to pursue timely resolution of problem institutions. This may involve difficult decisions, such as the use of supervisory and legal authorities to resolve a bank when some amount of book capital remains but it has become reasonably clear that the bank is no longer viable and additional rehabilitative efforts are futile. Examiners dealing with these issues must consult with their supervisory office, policy and legal experts and, in many cases, senior management of the OCC and the other federal banking agencies.

Since the mid-1990s the banking system has prospered. The number of problem banks is low, and bank failures are rare. However, history has shown that a bank's condition can deteriorate quickly. An FDIC study indicates that of the banks that failed between 1980 and 1994, 36 percent were CAMEL rated "1" or "2" within two years of failure.[3] This underscores the importance of early detection and timely resolution of supervisory concerns.

This section discusses some of the most common red flags and identifiers of problems and the early warning systems and other monitoring tools that can identify them. It also describes documentation and communication expectations for OCC personnel.

I.   Red Flags and Other Identifiers

Red flags and identifiers of problem banks take many forms and require examiners to consider a number of diverse factors before determining the most appropriate supervisory response. The following subsections outline critical identifiers, provide additional sources of information, and suggest courses of action for problems uncovered.

---

[3]   FDIC, *History of the Eighties — Lessons for the Future, p. 59.*

A. Rapid Growth/Aggressive Growth Strategies

Pursuit of aggressive growth in the 1980s and early 1990s stretched many banks' management teams and increased their exposure to risks. This led to numerous and sometimes sudden failures as sectoral economic conditions changed, *e.g.*, in energy and real estate. Thus, even when banks are apparently in good health, examiners should always closely evaluate rapid growth strategies for vulnerability to management gaps and economic downturns.

Excessive growth, particularly as measured against local, regional, and national economic indicators, has long been viewed as a potential precursor to credit quality problems. Such growth can strain bank underwriting and risk selection standards, as well as the capacity of management, existing internal control structures and administrative processes. Excessive growth may also reflect fundamental changes in bank practices warranting additional supervisory attention. Changes in bank practices evidenced by excessive growth include changes in underwriting and pricing standards, revisions to customer/product risk tolerances, increased anxiety for income, introduction of unbalanced compensation programs, and expansion of, or changes to, lending areas or sources of loans. Obviously, aggressive growth will also serve to exacerbate problems at a bank with pre-existing risk management deficiencies.

When performing supervisory activities at a bank experiencing rapid growth, examiners must investigate closely the institution's circumstances and alter supervisory plans, if one or more of the following conditions exist:

- Growth varies significantly from the bank's budget or strategic plan.
- Risk profile is higher than anticipated.
- Bank underwriting and risk selection standards have been revised.
- Minimal or no changes have been made to the bank's internal control structures.
- Capital levels are declining rapidly.
- Funding sources are unstable or short-term.
- New products and activities are being pursued with little or no expertise or with inadequate risk management controls.
- Growth is influenced heavily by brokered or agent transactions.

A number of sources exist to help examiners monitor a bank's growth. Many of the recently established Canary Benchmark Ratios are designed to assist field examiners in identifying banks with rates of growth warranting additional review. For example, Canary focuses on banks whose total loans and leases have increased beyond a threshold percentage since the same quarter in the previous year. The Uniform Bank Performance Report (UBPR) also highlights rapid changes in major categories during the previous quarter and provides annual comparisons. In addition, the "Snapshot Report" in the Assistant Deputy Comptroller (ADC) Report Package includes asset growth information. Moreover, some of the most meaningful information about bank growth and projections frequently can be found in bank budgets, operating plans, and strategic plans.

Appendix A provides additional guidance for supervising banks that are experiencing rapid growth.

B. Deterioration in the Economy

A clear correlation exists between bank performance and economic conditions in the markets served. In the 1980s, the collapse of energy prices, followed by real estate values, played a significant role in failures throughout the Southwest and the West. In the early 1990s, the sharp decline in real estate values in the Northeast led to deterioration in many banks throughout that region and contributed to the failure of several institutions.

Examiners must remain aware of the effect of local, national, and global economies on significant bank lines of business. This is not an easy task, as many banks operate several lines of business crossing multiple geographies, and, therefore, can be affected by a variety of factors.

Researching economic information can be time-consuming for examiners. A number of economic tools, however, are available to obtain information about economic indicators. For an efficient search, examiners will need a general understanding of the specific economic indicators affecting the bank most directly. Examples of some common economic indicators are:

- Bankruptcies.
- Business failures.
- Employment.
- Consumer delinquency rates.
- Existing home prices.
- Gross domestic product.
- Market prices.
- Income.
- Inflation rates.
- Industrial vacancy rates.
- Interest rates.
- Office vacancies.
- Real estate absorption rates.
- Trade deficit.
- Wages and salaries.
- Country risks.

In some cases, examiners may need more specific economic information. For example, if concerns about a particular industry arise (*e.g.*, agriculture), examiners may consider reviewing:

- Industry studies (*e.g.*, agribusiness).
- National or District Risk Committee information (*e.g.*, Western states export sales).
- Trade data (*e.g.*, USDA crop price reports).
- Local publications.

Several sources are available within the OCC to help examiners obtain timely economic information important to the problem bank identification process. For example, examiners can easily obtain many of the economic indicators mentioned through the Haver Regional Economic

Focus system. The Canary Web site's Market Barometers contain indicators that provide a broad sense of liquidity in the capital markets, perceptions on credit risk, and a general view of public confidence. The Market Spillover tools in Canary enable examiners to investigate the direct and indirect linkages between an individual bank and the markets in which it operates. The Commercial Real Estate Web site contains analysis, data, and forecasts on national and local commercial real estate markets and analyses of Real Estate Investment Trusts.

Other analytical tools also are available. For specific industry studies, examiners can obtain Standard and Poor's industry surveys through the Industry Section Information Service (ISIS). Haver and ISIS are accessible through intranet links located within the Economics and Policy Analysis Home Pages and within the ADC Toolkit application. Banking industry reports are available on the intranet links located within the National Risk Committee's Home Page. Country-specific news and analysis reports and other international data are available through intranet links located within the International Banking and Finance Home Page. Other studies prepared by OCC staff are contained within the Special Studies section of the ADC Toolkit application. Examiners may also request specific information by contacting a district risk analyst or through the OCC Library. In addition, specific economic information relevant to a particular bank's product lines often can be obtained through discussions with bank management and in-house economists and through studies prepared for the bank.

Examiners should use this and other supervisory information to determine the potential exposure of the bank to deteriorating economic conditions. In making this determination, examiners should:

- Assess the adequacy of the bank's capital and ALLL to cover lower earnings and increased loan losses.
- Review the bank's loan portfolio to identify loans with structural weaknesses and concentrations in vulnerable economic sectors or borrowers.
- Evaluate the bank's interest rate risk exposure, including any unrealized portfolio depreciation and potential asset extensions or liability contractions due to embedded balance sheet options.
- Ensure the bank has adequate liquidity and contingency funding plans to cover potential market disruptions or deposit run-offs.

After reviewing relevant economic information and identifying concerns about a bank or a group of banks, examiners should focus supervisory efforts on those product lines and areas that pose the greatest risk. But prior to developing a supervisory plan, examiners should discuss economic concerns with bank management to obtain their perspective on the risks to the bank(s) and planned courses of action, if any, to address such risks.

Examiners must be especially vigilant in monitoring potential risk exposures and ensuring that banks are taking appropriate remedial actions during the latter stage of a business cycle. It is during this stage — while earnings are still strong and management attention is not diverted to problem management — that corrective actions are likely to be most successful and least costly. The formality of OCC actions will vary, depending upon the severity of a bank's problems and management's ability and willingness to address those problems. Deteriorating economic conditions, when coupled with a bank's failure to address previously identified weaknesses, generally will warrant more forceful supervisory corrective action.

C. Management Oversight Deficiencies

Although economic conditions are a major influence on a bank's well being, management is the dominant factor. Decisions made today can have far-reaching implications on a bank's future condition, and a strong manager will take steps to avoid or mitigate the severity of possible adverse economic forces. Many of the bank failures that occurred in the 1980s and early 1990s can be attributed primarily to poor management decisions. [4] Because of the direct effect managers and directors have on a bank's health, examiners must pay particular attention to indicators of oversight or management deficiencies. Some examples are:

- *Non-responsive management.* Failure by bank management to take corrective action can result quickly in the deterioration of the bank's condition. Therefore, management's non-responsiveness to recommendations warrants close evaluation by examiners. Examiners should pay particular attention to remedial actions when following up on Matters Requiring Attention (MRAs), violations of law, or responses to audit criticisms.

- *Passive or uniformed board of directors.* A strong, independent, and knowledgeable board contributes to the long-term health of any bank, and during difficult economic times, a strong board may be required for the bank's survival. The board of directors should set the overall tone and direction of the bank and establish guidelines for the nature and amount of risk the bank may take. This requires effective oversight of bank management and ensuring that adequate controls and systems are in place to identify and manage risks and address problems. Directors should also remain up-to-date on key banking activities, particularly new ones for the bank to ensure prudent decision-making.

- *Increasing noncompliance with laws or internal standards.* Increased frequency of noncompliance with laws, regulations, or bank policies and practices is a symptom of slippage in controls and compliance systems. Compliance defects can expose the bank to operational losses, fines, civil money penalties, payment of damages, and the voiding of contracts. Examiners should be alert for trends in violations and exceptions, as well as significant litigation resulting from these problems. Often, compliance weaknesses are accompanied by other problems within the bank, such as irregular insider activities, audit deficiencies, and inadequate MIS.

- *Insufficient planning and response to risks.* A weak planning process and the inability to respond to industry changes will expose a bank to additional strategic risk. Examiners should be alert for a lack of long-term planning, conflicting organizational goals, inadequate resources to achieve goals, and inadequate implementation plans. For banks pursuing new activities, examiners should review their analysis of the risks and rewards of such activities. Examiners should also discuss the bank's future plans and management's alternatives, should assumptions not materialize (*e.g.*, growth rates and profit levels).

---

[4] An OCC bank failure study completed in 1988 concluded that management-driven weaknesses played a significant role in 90 percent of the cases reviewed.

- *Inadequate talent and experience at the CEO level.* The CEO has a major effect on the success or failure of a bank. Therefore, examiners should be knowledgeable about a CEO's professional experience, particularly in managing under adverse conditions and the specific expertise he or she provides to the bank. Examiners also should make a careful assessment of the CEO's abilities to provide leadership and to manage the bank. Banks entering new activities or expanding through internal growth or mergers and acquisitions may challenge a CEO's abilities. Therefore, examiners must assess the abilities of all members of executive management.

Lapses or weaknesses in managerial oversight should be noted in examination reports and commitments should be obtained from the bank's board or senior management for corrective action. If previously identified problems have not been addressed satisfactorily, examiners should reconfirm the appropriateness of previous recommendations, evaluate the board's and management's commitment, and proceed with incremental action consistent with the severity of the problem.

D. Inappropriate Limits on OCC Access to Bank Staff and Documents

By statute (12 USC 481 and 1867), examiners are entitled to prompt and unrestricted access to the books, records, and staff of national banks and their servicers. A denial of such access should be a red flag to examiners. Although such a situation may reflect merely a lack of understanding on the part of management, it may also indicate that the bank is attempting to conceal evidence of violations of law or unsafe or unsound practices or prevent examiners from discovering the bank's true financial condition.

Examiners should be aware of the following red flags, indicating an intent to deny timely and complete access to information:

- Refusal to provide information within a reasonable time period.
- Use of agents, such as bank counsel, to prescreen requests for examination documents.
- Alteration of records prior to examiner review.
- Unexplained disappearance of key records.
- Blocking access to relevant third-party records.
- Attack on the credibility of individual examiners.

When encountering situations like the ones previously noted, examiners should contact their supervisory office immediately. In many cases the situation may be a simple misunderstanding that can be resolved quickly. However, if access is not secured or the situation resolved within a reasonably brief period, the supervisory office should contact the appropriate OCC Law Department staff for assistance. In general in such situations, the particular circumstances of the denial of access should be documented in writing, and a written request for access sent to the bank. The request should note that failure to comply with the information request will be deemed concealment of, and refusal to submit, the bank's books and records for purposes of the OCC's enforcement and receivership authority. Additional specific guidance for these situations is contained in PPM 5310-10, "Guidance to Examiners in Securing Access to Bank Books and Records," dated January 7, 2000.

E. Risk Management Deficiencies

Sound risk management systems can mitigate risk assumed by a bank. As illustrated in the 1980s and early 1990s, banks with well-developed risk management systems were less likely to fail than banks with weak systems. All risk management systems should identify, measure, monitor and control risk. Although the structure of risk management systems will vary from bank to bank, when assessing risk management, examiners should consider a bank's:

- *Policies* (*e.g.*, internal standards, risk tolerance limits)
- *Processes* (*e.g.*, internal controls, periodic audits, validation testing)
- *Personnel* (*e.g.*, management, expertise, staffing levels, training)
- *Controls* (*e.g.*, audit, management information systems)

Because deficiencies in risk management can exist in any area of the bank, each member of an examination team should be knowledgeable about the quality of policies, processes, personnel, and control systems within his or her assigned area(s). Some examples of risk management deficiencies include:

- A loan policy that is not well defined or well understood.
- An internal audit program that lacks independence.
- Interest rate risk measurement tools that are too simplistic for the size and complexity of on- and off-balance-sheet exposures.
- Management that does not anticipate emerging technology needs.
- Acquisition due diligence processes that do not consider the risks associated with new products and compatibility with corporate goals.

If significant risk management deficiencies accompany increasing or high levels of risk, examiners should step up the intensity of supervisory activities and communications with management and directors until the situation is resolved. In this context, examiner recommendations and expectations must be clear, specific, and directly relevant to the conditions at hand. Ambiguous admonitions about the need for improvement seldom produce the desired results. More formal supervisory responses generally will be warranted when risk management deficiencies are coupled with other red flags, such as rapid growth or deteriorating economic conditions.

F. Significant Off-Balance-Sheet Exposure

The volume of off-balance-sheet activities for national banks has risen significantly since the last banking crisis. Although off-balance-sheet exposures were not a primary cause of bank failures in the past, they increasingly warrant examiner attention. With the increase in bank securitization activity and the proliferation of capital markets products, more and more credit risk is shifting to off-balance-sheet transactions. Traditionally, off-balance-sheet credit risk has come primarily from loan commitments and letters of credit. The credit risk in these products is fairly straightforward. The credit risk inherent in capital markets products, such as asset securitizations and derivatives, however, is more difficult to quantify, because of the need to assign a credit risk equivalent. Examiners should include an assessment of off-balance-sheet and any other indirect exposures when determining the overall quantity of risk assumed by the bank.

Asset Securitization

Asset securitization involves the transfer of on-balance-sheet assets to a third party, normally a trust, partnership, or other special purpose vehicle (SPV), which then issues "asset-backed securities" to investors. The repayment of the asset-backed securities is supported by the cash flows of the transferred assets. If used properly, asset securitization can provide important benefits to banks. Securitization allows banks to allocate capital more efficiently, access diverse and cost-effective funding sources, and better manage business risks. It may also improve profitability. However, if not used properly and managed effectively, asset securitization may materially increase risk to the bank.

Financial Accounting Standard 125, "Accounting for Transfers and Servicing of Financial Assets and Extinguishments of Liabilities" (FAS 125) governs the accounting treatment for asset transfers in a securitization transaction. If a securitization transaction meets FAS 125 criteria, the seller must recognize a gain or loss on the sale on the date of the transaction (known as "gain on sale accounting"). Future expected cash flow streams from securitized assets are recognized by establishing residual assets and servicing assets or liabilities.

The valuation methods and assumptions used to value the residuals and servicing assets are critical bank judgments that warrant supervisory attention. If conservative and realistic, these valuation methods and assumptions may provide a reasonable estimation of the value of future expected cash flows. However, even if valuations and assumptions are conservative and reasonable when made, they are only estimates. Actual performance of the underlying assets may differ from the original estimates, leading to write-downs and capital impairment. The advent of FAS 125 increases the potential for issuers to generate "paper profits" or mask actual losses through flawed assumptions, inaccurate prepayment rates, and unsupported discount rates. These practices can also lead to significant write-downs of the residual asset.

In addition, asset securitization transactions may explicitly or implicitly provide investors with recourse to the bank that can affect capital adversely. Therefore, a bank that engages in securitizations must be fully aware of relevant risk-based capital rules for those transactions.

Banks involved in asset securitization transactions must have appropriate risk management structures in place to monitor and control associated risk. For example, the board of directors and senior management should ensure that all valuation methods and key assumptions used to value the residuals and servicing assets and liabilities are reasonable, fully documented, and well supported. Effective internal controls and audit functions should also be in place for securitization activities. For additional information on supervisory issues in this area, see the "Asset Securitization" booklet of the *Comptroller's Handbook* and OCC Bulletin 99-46, "Interagency Guidance on Asset Securitization Activities" (December 16, 1999).

Derivatives

Financial derivatives are defined broadly as instruments that primarily derive their value from the performance of underlying interest or foreign exchange rates, equity, or commodity prices. Examples include futures, forwards, swaps, options, structured debt obligations and deposits and various combinations thereof. Risks associated with derivatives are basically the same as those faced in traditional activities (*e.g.*, price, interest rate, liquidity, and credit risk). Fundamentally, the risk of derivatives is a function of the timing and variability of cash flows.

Financial derivatives have specific risk-based capital requirements. The risk-based capital rules outline a two-step process of calculating the amount to be included in risk-weighted assets for a derivative. First the derivative must be converted to an on-balance-sheet credit equivalent amount.[5] Then the credit equivalent amount is multiplied by a risk weight[6] and included in risk-weighted assets. The risk weight may be reduced to recognize certain collateral or guarantees, such as cash or securities of the U.S. government, its agencies or the governments of Organization for Economic Cooperation and Development (OECD) countries.

Financial Accounting Standard 133, "Accounting for Derivative Instruments and Hedging Activities" (FAS 133), mandated that institutions record all derivatives on their balance sheets as assets or liabilities at fair value, effective January 2001. The accounting for changes in the fair value of a derivative (*i.e.*, gains and losses) depends on the intended use of the derivative. The accounting treatment prescribed in FAS 133 may affect a bank's leverage and risk-based capital ratios, and if a bank's volume of derivative activity is high, it could affect the bank's capital category for purposes of Prompt Corrective Action (PCA). (See the "Resolving Credit and Impairment Problems" section for a discussion of PCA.) OCC Bulletins 98-45 and 99-1 discuss in detail FAS 133 and the risk-based capital treatment for derivatives used for hedging activities.

Examiners who evaluate a bank's off-balance-sheet activities through ongoing monitoring, targeted activities, and core assessment examinations should check for potential increases in risk exposure to the bank. Examples of some general red flags for off-balance-sheet activities include:

- Participation in markets without appropriate knowledge or expertise.
- Large levels of off-balance-sheet activity relative to the bank's size and risk profile.
- Substantial exposure to a counterparty whose ongoing ability to meet its obligations is uncertain.
- Significant residual values or recourse obligations related to securitization transactions.
- Accounting errors for off-balance-sheet products.

---

[5] The credit equivalent amount of a derivative equals the fair value of the derivative (if it is positive) plus an additional amount for the potential future credit exposure. The additional amount for the potential future credit exposure is the notional amount of the derivative multiplied by a credit conversion factor that depends on the remaining maturity and type of contract (*e.g.*, interest rate, foreign exchange, equity or commodity).

[6] The risk weight is determined by criteria listed in Appendix A of 12 CFR 3 and depends, in part, on the type of counterparty.

- No established limits for off-balance-sheet activities.
- Underestimating the effect of off-balance-sheet products on the bank's risk-based capital position.
- Inadequate oversight mechanisms (audit, market risk, loan review and compliance).

If concerns arise, examiners should seek expert advice for that particular product. Contacts include the district capital markets experts and specialists and the staffs of Capital Policy, Treasury and Market Risk, and Risk Analysis at OCC headquarters.

Information on specific off-balance-sheet activities can be found in the "Asset Securitization," "Risk Management of Financial Derivatives," and "Interest Rate Risk" booklets of the *Comptroller's Handbook*. The Treasury and Market Risk division also has helpful links on its intranet home page that includes reference and analysis tools for off-balance-sheet products.

G. Asset Quality Deterioration

The most common financial risk shared by problem banks during the banking crisis of the 1980s and early 1990s was asset quality deterioration. Whether caused by economic factors, poor management, anxiety for earnings, insider abuse or other factors, poor asset quality was a factor in nearly all problem banks.

The following signals may point to asset quality deterioration. Listed first are indicators that may be accessed off-site from standardized sources, followed by indicators derived from communications with bankers and on-site examination.

Off-site Indicators
- Significant loan growth with or without increases in delinquencies, losses, or ALLL provisions.
- Increasing levels of past due and nonperforming loans as a percent of loans, either in aggregate or within loan types.
- Significant changes in the Allowance for Loan and Lease Losses (ALLL). (See the following section.)
- Increasing levels of Other Real Estate Owned (OREO).
- Increasing levels of Interest Earned Not Collected (IENC) as a percent of loans, particularly when compared with historical and peer levels.
- Deterioration in local economic conditions.
- High growth rates in overall loans or individual loan types, particularly subprime or high loan-to-value products.
- Increasing proportion of long-term loans.
- Exceeding various Canary credit risk benchmarks

On-site and Communication Indicators
- Increase in the bank's average risk ratings, loan classifications, special mention, or watch list credits.
- Large volume of policy and underwriting exceptions.
- Large volume of loans with structural weaknesses.

- Excessive credit/collateral documentation deficiencies.
- Inadequate or inaccurate MIS.
- Increased credit-related legal expenses.
- Significant changes in number or experience of lending or credit administration staff.
- Delinquent internal loan reviews.
- Inordinately high volume of out-of-area lending.
- Large or increasing volume of unsecured lending.
- Increasing concentrations.

The existence of one or more of these indicators should cause the examiner or supervisory office to ensure that the suspect area is targeted for specific and timely review and that steps for corrective action are underway. If a bank fails to implement remedial action in a timely manner, more forceful supervisory action should be taken.

H. Significant ALLL and Asset Valuation Adjustment Issues

Banks in stress may attempt to postpone recognition of problems by deferring loan loss provisions and chargeoffs. Therefore, examiners must be alert to symptoms that may indicate such tactics. The following are signals that merit closer review of the ALLL to ensure that it is adequate and that provisions are being made at acceptable levels.

- The rate of growth in the ALLL is significantly greater or less than the rate of growth in total loans over previous quarter(s) or previous one-year periods. A disproportionately large rate of growth in the ALLL might signal a significant increase in problem loans. Conversely, if the rate of loan growth significantly exceeds that of the ALLL, it might signal an attempt to manipulate earnings at the expense of maintaining ALLL adequacy.

- The percentage of nonperforming or classified loans to total loans is increasing at a greater rate than the ALLL.

- Net loan loss coverage is low. Frequently-used benchmarks are quarterly net loan losses that are 15 percent or greater than the beginning ALLL, or 60 percent or greater annually.

- The documentation for quarterly analysis of ALLL adequacy does not indicate appropriate consideration of adjustments for historical loss experience. As discussed in the "Allowance for Loan and Lease Losses" booklet of the *Comptroller's Handbook*, the following factors may warrant adjustments to the ALLL:
  - Changes in lending policies and procedures, including underwriting, collection, charge-off, and recovery policies.
  - Changes in national and local economic and business conditions, including individual market and industry segments.
  - Changes in the nature and volume of the loan portfolio.
  - Changes in the experience, ability, and depth of lending management staff.
  - Changes in the volume and severity of past due and classified loans and in the volume of nonaccruals, troubled debt restructures, and other loan modifications.

- Changes in the quality of the bank's loan review system and the degree of oversight by the bank's board of directors.
- The existence and effect of any concentrations of credit and changes in the level of such concentrations.
- The effect of external factors, such as competition and legal and regulatory requirements, on the level of estimated credit losses in the bank's current portfolio.

The indicators previously discussed suggest only that the ALLL might be a problem. The examiner must view these indicators in conjunction with other factors, such as merger and acquisition activity, the quality of management, underwriting standards, the appetite for risk, credit systems and controls, risk rating accuracy and timeliness, the institution's propensity to manage earnings, and historical allowance adequacy (*e.g.*, the track record of maintaining adequacy at minimum or maximum levels).

The examiner also should test to ensure that valuations of problem assets are reasonable. Often in a problem situation, bank management will attempt to inflate collateral values to avoid loss recognition. In practice, this is most often accomplished by postponing recognition that the value of the collateral has declined. The most efficient method of testing collateral valuation is to review appraisals or other valuations on several large problem loans and OREO holdings. Normally, if valuation is a problem, it will be apparent in the largest collateral dependent problem assets. Doubtful assets should be reviewed first. Guidance on collateral valuation is provided in various credit-related booklets of the *Comptroller's Handbook.*

I. Strained Liquidity

Historically, bank liquidity crises could be mitigated and liquidity failures sometimes avoided by sustained funding through the Federal Reserve Discount Window. With the passage of FDICIA, however, Discount Window borrowings are much more limited, especially for banks that are less than adequately capitalized by FDICIA standards. Therefore, examiners must be even more keenly aware of situations that may have an adverse impact on a bank's ability to obtain funding. Funding constraints can be precipitated by numerous causes, including deterioration in a bank's financial condition, fraud, or external economic events. A bank's liquidity situation may also become compromised if its reputation "on the street" is suspect either due to real or perceived shortfalls. In any event, the extent of a potential funding problem depends on the risk tolerance of a bank's funds providers.

Examiners must gain an understanding of a bank's funds providers and its funds management strategy before making judgments on the bank's liquidity position. This is important because retail and wholesale fund providers have different credit and interest rate sensitivities and will react differently to changes in economic and bank conditions. Retail funds providers, generally insured public depositors, historically have not been very credit- or interest rate-sensitive. In contrast, wholesale funds providers — typically other financial institutions, governmental units, large commercial and industrial corporations, or wealthy individuals — are usually placed by professionals and are generally very credit- and interest rate-sensitive.

With that in mind, examiners should be aware of the red flags that may signal potential liquidity strain and a need for additional analysis, monitoring, and contingency planning. Examples of such indicators are:

- Low levels of on-hand liquidity (*i.e.,* money market assets and net unpledged marketable investment securities).
- Significant increases in large CDs, brokered deposits, or deposits with above-market interest rates, particularly in banks that have been heavily retail-funded.
- Significant increases in borrowings, warehouse lines, and Federal Home Loan Bank lines (assuming no seasonality).
- Funding mismatches (*i.e.,* funding long-term assets with short-term liabilities).
- Higher costs of funds relative to the market.
- Reduction in borrowing lines by correspondent banks.
- Counterparty requests for collateral to secure borrowing lines.
- Declines in core deposit levels.
- Sudden drop in bank's stock price.
- Downgrades of credit rating by rating agencies.
- Withdrawal of funds by rating-sensitive providers, such as trust managers, money managers, and public entities.
- Unwillingness of counterparties and brokers to deal in off-balance-sheet or longer dated transactions.

Numerous sources of information may assist examiners in identifying liquidity red flags. These sources include the UBPR, sources and uses reports, the bank's contingency funding plan, concentration reports, liquidity trend reports, liquidity risk focus reports (Canary intranet home page), market reports (internet), and the Large Bank Liquidity Watch Report (Treasury and Market Risk intranet home page). Discussions with management may also provide examiners with valuable information about the risk tolerance and credit sensitivity of funds providers and an estimate of projected funding the bank will lose given various scenarios.

If examiners discover a potential liquidity problem, they should contact their supervisor and, depending on the severity of the problem, consult a capital markets specialist or expert to determine the appropriate course of action. Since liquidity problems can worsen quickly as the risk tolerance of funds providers shrink, timely action is critical.

J. Insider Abuse and Fraud

Insider abuse and fraud have been contributing factors in many bank failures. Such conduct can quickly affect a bank's condition and undermine public confidence even in banks that are otherwise in sound condition. Financial institution fraud can occur throughout a bank's operations and is usually accompanied by a lack of oversight and controls. Some actions that constitute financial fraud include:[7]

---

[7]   Fraud Examiners Manual, 1993 Association of Certified Fraud Examiners, p. 1.1005

- A dishonest or fraudulent act.
- Forgery or alteration of documents.
- Misapplication of funds or assets.
- Impropriety in reporting financial transactions.
- Profiting from insider knowledge.
- Disclosing securities transactions to others.
- Accepting gifts from vendors.

Fraud and abuse typically are concealed from *routine* scrutiny; however, as with other types of problems, there usually are symptoms that can aid in detection. During on-site examinations, examiners should be aware of any transactions with insiders and their related interests that may indicate preferential treatment, a breach of fiduciary duty, personal gain or other breach of Regulation O. Some examples of suspect transactions with insiders include:

- Excessive salaries, bonuses, and fees relative to the size and condition of the bank.
- Fees paid when there is no benefit to the bank (*e.g.*, personal legal fees).
- Fees paid for services not yet received (*e.g.*, an advance to an insider's company for future rehabilitation work on other real estate owned properties).
- Fees established solely to meet a shareholder's or insider-related organization's need for funds (*e.g.*, a monthly consulting fee paid to a director experiencing financial difficulties).
- Extensions of credit granted on more favorable terms (*e.g.*, a lower interest rate on the president's loan when compared with those for similar borrowers).
- Higher rates paid on insider deposits (*e.g.*, higher interest rates offered to an insider's company).
- Unexplained or irregular transactions between insiders and bank customers or bank affiliates.
- Unreasonable refusal of bank officers to provide access to bank or bank-related records or information deemed relevant by examiners.
- Efforts by bank officers to obstruct access to relevant information.

Because of the nature of OCC's on-site work, one of the most common types of fraud uncovered by examiners is loan fraud. Loan fraud can take many forms; *e.g.*, loans can be made to fictitious parties or granted with false credit and financial information. Loans can also involve kickbacks and diversion of funds. As examiners perform credit analysis on a loan-by-loan and portfolio basis, they should be alert to the following red flags that may signal potential loan fraud:[8]

- Large volumes of loans replaced rapidly in a portfolio.
- Low quality assets sold to affiliated and unaffiliated banks.
- Missing documentation and other support for draw requests.
- Inflated real estate appraisals, especially when an above-market appraisal fee is paid.
- Unexplained cost overruns on construction loans.
- Rapid sales and purchases of land by borrower within a short time frame.

---

[8]   Fraud Examiners Manual, 1993 Association of Certified Fraud Examiners, pp.1.1114 - 1.1119, 1.1134-35

- Numerous loan increases and extensions without justification.
- Unexplained cash flow discrepancies.

The policy for obtaining certain bank examination information produced by third parties was changed recently. This came about because a national bank was able to manipulate information from its loan servicer prior to submitting it to examiners and the increasing reliance on third parties for loan servicing and asset securitization. Under our new policy, loan and asset securitization trial balance information must be requested directly from the bank's servicer. By receiving the information directly, the OCC minimizes the possibility that a bank may manipulate the data.

Fraud also can take many forms in the operations area. Large or uncollected funds balances may signal check-kiting schemes. New accounts may be opened with forged or stolen checks. Wires may include fraudulent transfer of funds. Uncontrolled access to critical systems may result in computer fraud.

Examiners should pay special attention to internal and external audit report conclusions on internal controls and separation of duties. Validation of a bank's internal and external audit program in conjunction with its control environment must occur every supervisory cycle, guided by the core assessment standards. Examiners use a progressive three-step process to validate the bank's audit program, commencing with a work paper review. If the required audit workpaper review identifies significant discrepancies or weaknesses in the audit program or the control environment, examiners will expand the examination of those areas and any affected operational or functional business area. Examiners will use internal control questionnaires in conjunction with the expanded procedures. If concerns remain, examiners should perform verification procedures to the extent necessary to resolve the concerns.

If insider abuse or fraud is detected or suspected, examiners should immediately advise their supervisors and district counsel who will decide whether to arrange for district or headquarters fraud experts to participate in the examination. Early contact with fraud experts is encouraged. Depending on the conclusions reached, remedial measures may include enforcement actions, civil money penalties, and/or referral to another agency.

II. Early Warning Systems and Monitoring Tools

The use of early warning systems and other monitoring tools is essential in bank supervision. These models, screens, filters, and other reports assist examiners in identifying trends in a bank or group of banks that may signal a problem. This information helps examiners monitor activities and trends and plan future examination activities and the scope of those activities. For example, financial ratios relative to asset quality may indicate inconsistency with the current asset quality component rating and warrant changes to the scope of the commercial loan review. Early warning and monitoring tools may also be used effectively during targets and examinations to verify or supplement findings. For example, the risk-based capital model may assist in identifying errors in the bank's assignment of risk weights that in turn may affect capital levels significantly.

A. Canary Early Warning Tools

The OCC recently introduced the Canary early warning tools to enhance the OCC's assessment of risk, both in individual banks and on a systemic basis. Canary brings under one Web site the diverse array of supervisory and economic predictive models and tools used throughout the OCC. The Canary Web site organizes early warning tools into four components: Benchmarks, Credit Scope, Market Barometers, and Predictive Models.

- Benchmarks are the most fundamental Canary early warning tools and, collectively, represent the core set of OCC analytical tools that examiners will use during on-site and off-site supervisory activities. These benchmarks facilitate early warning analysis by highlighting high credit, interest rate, and liquidity positions and identifying banks that may need additional supervisory analysis.

- Credit Scope includes a series of tools to assist examiners in assessing credit risk. The Credit Assessment Tool (discussed more fully later) is directly accessible from Canary, as are the most recent KMV analyses and Loan Concentration Tool. KMV is a predicative tool that provides information about the level of credit risk within the universe of publicly traded companies. The Loan Concentration Tool is used to produce a list of all loan concentrations by SIC code in a bank as of its last examination, or conversely, to produce a list of banks concentrated in a selected SIC code. Credit Scope also includes a link to the Commercial Real Estate Web site.

- Market Barometers provide a broad view of perceived credit risk, expected interest rate movements, overall liquidity in the financial markets and consumer confidence and wealth.

- Predictive Models include several models to assist examiners in assessing the future effects of existing risk positions on bank performance. These tools include PGRM (Peer Group Risk Models), the FDIC's SCOR (Statistical CAMELS Off-site Ratings), and Bank Risk Calculator. PGRM is a series of econometric models designed to project the potential impact of different economic scenarios on future ratings for similar asset-based bank peer groups. SCOR, using 13 financial ratios, forecasts composite and component ratings and assigns a probability that the institution's CAMELS ratings will be downgraded. Bank Risk Calculator is an analytical tool that uses Call Report data and unemployment rates for bank market areas to classify the overall risk in individual and groups of small banks.

In addition to the Canary early warning tools, examiners may find a variety of other tools useful. These tools are described in the section below. However, neither Canary nor other forms of off-site analytical tools replace the critical roles of examiner experience and judgment. Although models and monitoring tools can aggregate financial data and, in some cases, draw preliminary conclusions on this data, examiners must verify a red flag or early warning signal and develop definitive conclusions on the effect on the bank.

B. Other Analytical Tools

- The "BERT Review and Risk Assessments Report" highlights negative trends within

CAMELS ratings, risk assessment factors, and BERT scores for an ADC's portfolio of banks. Negative trends in a bank's BERT scores and risk assessments without corresponding changes in the CAMELS ratings could signal potential deterioration that should be further reviewed. This report is part of the ADC Report Package that is distributed quarterly by the district financial analysts. For additional information, examiners may contact the Supervisory Data staff or assigned district financial analyst.

- Bank Performance Projection Model (BPPM) is designed for problem bank cases, when ultimate bank solvency may be in question. By programming various scenarios, such as projected capital levels, OREO losses, and provision expenses, examiners can view a snapshot of future performance and compare it with current and past performance. This tool is especially useful when trends are negative, but are not yet recognized by management or the board. BPPM is available via the LAN. For additional information, examiners may contact the Core Policy Development staff.

- Credit Assessment Tool (CAT) is an analytical tool that uses Call Report information to classify individual and groups of banks with respect to their current credit quality condition and potential to develop problems over the next year or two. CAT uses an examiner-friendly screening/scoring paradigm and generally accepted indicators of bank condition and performance. This tool is helpful in conducting ongoing monitoring activities when credit quality may be an issue. CAT is available through the ADC Toolkit. For additional information, examiners may contact the Economics Department.

- GRAPH is a model that provides a graphic comparison of selected NBSVDS data (*e.g.*, profitability factors, ALLL ratios, and growth rates) for the bank and its peers. The graphs are a quick and effective way to illustrate concerns about performance or trends, especially when the bank is an outlier compared with its peers. Use of these graphs may enhance communications with the board during meetings or in the report of examination. GRAPH is available through the LAN. For additional information, examiners may contact the Core Policy Development staff.

- The Risk Based Capital Model (RBCAP) provides a uniform and consistent estimate of risk based capital ratios and enables simulation analysis and evaluation of expected changes to capital, assets, and off-balance-sheet items. This can be helpful, not only in determining compliance with capital regulations, but also in evaluating a bank's capital plan. RBCAP is available through the LAN. For additional information, examiners may contact the Core Policy Development staff.

- The Rating Summary/Changes Report highlights downgrades and upgrades for composite, CAMELS, and specialty ratings for banks within an ADC's portfolio. This report can be especially helpful in identifying problem specialty areas that can affect the CAMELS composite and management ratings. This report is part of the ADC Report Package distributed quarterly by the district financial analysts. For additional information, examiners may contact the Supervisory Data staff or assigned district financial analyst.

- The National Bank Rank Ordering Report (NBROR) is a monitoring tool designed to identify community and mid-size banks whose financial ratios appear to be inconsistent with current CAMELS ratings. The report is divided into various sections that may highlight the worst performers in a given category, such as earnings. This report is useful in comparing a group of banks on a national basis, within a district, or within an ADC's portfolio. The Supervisory Data unit distributes the NBROR to the District Deputy Comptrollers, District Financial Analysts, and members of senior management. For additional information, examiners may contact the Supervisory Data staff.

III. Documentation of Supervisory Risks in Problem Banks

It is not unusual for examiner conclusions and enforcement actions relating to problem banks to be challenged by bank management and/or directors. For that reason, examiners must take extra care in fully documenting in writing their work and decision processes in problem banks. This documentation is important in providing support for corrective action and, if later required, receivership.

Documentation also includes ensuring that appropriate ratings have been assigned under the OCC's Risk Assessment System (RAS) and the uniform interagency rating system (CAMELS). These evaluation systems provide information about a bank's:

- Overall soundness.
- Financial and operational weaknesses or adverse trends.
- Problems or deteriorating conditions.
- Risk management practices.

Because of their commonalities, RAS and CAMELS can and do affect one another. For example, examiners may rate credit risk in a bank with increasing adverse trends and weak risk management practices as "moderate and increasing" or "high and increasing." Such a RAS rating normally should influence the CAMELS component rating for asset quality downward, if the current rating does not already reflect the appropriate level of supervisory concern. When the two rating systems are used in this manner, they provide an important verification of early warning tools and planned activities.

The major distinction between the RAS and CAMELS lies within their prospective vs. point-in-time distinctions. Although CAMELS now includes an assessment of the quality of risk management practices, it remains primarily a point-in-time assessment of its component factors. The RAS provides an expanded method of identifying, evaluating, documenting, and communicating examiner judgment about the quantity of all categories of risk, the quality of risk management, and the direction of risk. If used correctly, the RAS provides, not only a current measurement of risk, but also a prospective view of the institution's risk profile, which is valuable in developing supervisory plans for problem banks.

A. Risk Assessment System

For the RAS to work as intended, examiners must not only have a clear understanding of general concepts of risk and risk management, but also must recognize the distinctions among classifications within individual risks. For example, when assessing the quantity of risk, examiners must make a determination as to whether risk is *low*, *moderate*, or *high*. When judging risk management, examiners should readily distinguish between *strong, satisfactory* or *weak* risk management systems. When examiners assess the direction of risk (*i.e., increasing, decreasing,* or *stable*), this judgment should be based on the expected trend given known conditions at the time of the assessment. When making their assessments, examiners should not avoid difficult decisions by using a "middle of the road" classification; doing so prevents accurate risk assessments. Use of the full range of these classifications will result in more precise risk assessments, which are critical in problem bank situations, because they drive supervisory strategies.

Examiners should consider the following factors when completing a RAS:

- *What is the overall trend of risk in the bank based on the risk assessment — increasing or decreasing?* Reviewing the trend of risk over several years can provide useful information in assessing a bank's supervisory history. In addition, a consistent increase or decrease in risk should prompt a review of the supervisory plan for the bank (*i.e.*, ratchet up supervisory focus for increased risk and pare it down for decreased risk).

- *Have changes in the risk assessment of the bank occurred as a result of ongoing supervision and monitoring activities?* The assessments are meant to be fluid, so an appropriate supervisory plan is in place for the institution. New information obtained through ongoing monitoring may warrant a change in the assessment of individual risks. An on-site examination is not required to change components of the risk assessment system.

- *In reviewing the direction of risk, have risks been designated as increasing for several periods?* If yes, has the assessment of "increasing" been accompanied by a change in the classification (*i.e.*, from low to moderate or moderate to high)? Although there are no specific policy guidelines that govern the maximum length of time a risk can be defined as "increasing," it is reasonable to surmise that after several periods of a "moderate and increasing" designation, the risk would progress to "high" and either "stable" or "increasing."

- *Has the full range of options within classifications been considered? In reviewing the results of the entire risk assessment, are all designations the same for the quantity of risk and the quality of risk management (or aggregate risk)?* If yes, a review of the facts supporting each rating may be beneficial, particularly if the only the middle classification (*i.e.*, moderate, satisfactory) is being used. As stated above, the use of the full range of risk assessment classifications will result in more precise risk assessments that are critical for problem bank supervisory strategies.

- *Has the quantity of risk exposure been appropriately weighed against risk management practices when determining aggregate risk?* For example, strong risk management practices may mitigate high or moderate risk levels and result in moderate or low aggregate risk assessment. Conversely, weak risk management practices will generally increase aggregate risk.

B. Uniform Interagency Rating Systems

For the CAMELS rating system to work as intended, examiners need a clear understanding of individual risk assessments and the bank's risk profile when assigning component and composite ratings. The effect of risk assessments on component ratings depends largely on aggregate risk and direction of risk. In addition, examiners must recognize the interrelationships that exist among component ratings while assigning ratings. For example, the level of problem assets is a primary consideration in assigning the asset quality component rating, but also should be considered in the capital and earnings ratings.

Some factors for examiners to consider when assigning ratings under the CAMELS or ROCA[9] systems include:

- *What is the general trend of risk in the bank? Overall are risks increasing or decreasing?* Trend analysis of a bank's ratings in conjunction with the risk assessments will provide useful information about supervisory history. A consistent increase or decrease in risk without a corresponding change in ratings should prompt a review of the supervisory plan for the bank.

- *Have changes in the ratings components occurred as a result of ongoing supervision and monitoring activities?* As risk assessments, ratings are meant to be fluid. New information obtained through ongoing monitoring may warrant a change in a component or composite rating. An on-site examination is not required to change rating components.

- *Have the interrelationships of other component ratings been given the appropriate weight?* Widespread credit management deficiencies at one bank may cause a downgrade to not only its management rating but to other components such as asset quality or liquidity. Weaknesses in interest rate risk management at another bank, however, may affect only the sensitivity to market risk rating.

IV. Communicating Concerns

Effective, accurate, and frequent communication with the board and management and other regulators is extremely important in problem bank supervision. It can also be one of the most difficult aspects of an examiner's job. Examiners must communicate in a manner reflective of the severity of a given situation. Communicating too harshly or not firmly enough can threaten the timely resolution of problems and compromise future communications.

A. Communicating Potential or Significant Problems

As examiners identify potential problems, they should routinely inform management and the board of preliminary findings. Doing so can ensure full identification and knowledge of the problem, speed up the resolution process, and prevent "surprises" when preliminary ratings are

---

[9] ROCA is the rating system used to evaluate the condition of a foreign banking organization's branch or agency. ROCA stands for risk management, operational controls, compliance, and asset quality.

disclosed during the exit meeting. When the potential problem is not serious, examiners should consider using moral suasion to effect corrective action. This approach can be particularly effective, if both the benefits of taking action and the consequences of inaction are presented persuasively to management.

Discussion of potential problems in the report of examination (ROE) or other written communication through the MRA section is another way of highlighting supervisory concerns. MRAs should address bank practices that "deviate from sound fundamental principles and are likely to result in financial deterioration if not addressed," or that "result in substantive noncompliance with laws." OCC senior management encourages the use of MRAs as a way to communicate the early identification of emerging issues and the critical need for follow up.

As examiners identify significant problems that affect the bank adversely, they must discuss them with management and the board as soon as practical. Examiners should be prepared for a range of reactions, from outright denial to complete acceptance. During these meetings, bank management must be allowed to clarify legitimate misunderstandings and commit to corrective action.

B. Conducting Exit Meetings in a Problem Bank Situation

At the conclusion of an examination or review, an exit meeting should be held with senior bank management and, in some cases, directors, to summarize conclusions, required corrective action, and planned OCC follow-up, including enforcement action, if any. This is an opportunity for the examiner to reaffirm conclusions that may have been discussed earlier in the examination, but that need refreshing or updating. In some cases, a representative of the supervisory office may attend the meeting to add emphasis.

Prior to the exit meeting, the EIC should have discussed significant findings, including ratings and recommendations for corrective action, with the appropriate supervisory office. Such a discussion helps ensure that OCC policy is applied consistently and that OCC management supports the conclusions and corrective action. This is particularly important in a problem bank situation, because management and the board often challenge conclusions, resist recommendations for corrective actions, or request additional information about noted concerns.

The EIC should prioritize issues during an exit meeting to aid management and directors in understanding the associated risk. A successful exit meeting will address both positive and negative aspects of the bank's condition and performance, but no ambiguity should exist about the most significant findings. If management deficiencies are the most important issues, it is often helpful to lead off with a discussion of other deficiencies to justify the conclusions about management. Without such an introduction, a discussion of management deficiencies can lead to a rancorous, defensive meeting. During the exit meeting, the OCC should seek and obtain commitments, including time frames, for corrective actions. Solutions proposed to effect correction should be appropriate for the size and complexity of the bank.

All final exit comments must be consistent, in tone and content, with written comments. Any intention to recommend an enforcement action should be communicated first verbally so that management is not surprised by subsequent written communications.

C. Conducting Board Meetings in a Problem Bank Situation

Meetings with the board of directors of a problem bank should be convened whenever there is material information to convey. Common topics include examination conclusions, future supervisory plans, corrective action updates, and presentation of enforcement actions. Ideally, the directors of a problem bank will be compelled by their sense of duty and responsibility to restore the bank to health, and in those cases, the meetings can be productive. Occasionally, however, the meetings are contentious and may prompt adoption of different supervisory and enforcement tactics.

Preparations for problem bank board meetings should be similar to those for exit meetings. (See also the "Bank Supervision Process" booklet of the *Comptroller's Handbook*.)

D. Communicating through the Report of Examination

The ROE is the OCC's standard, and usually the initial, formal communication of supervisory concerns to a bank. As such, it should clearly prioritize conclusions and problems in a way that also highlights any repeat deficiencies and non-compliance with prior commitments. The root causes of problems should be addressed, so that no ambiguity exists about responsibility for problems and required corrective actions.

Writing a ROE for problem banks is generally more challenging than ROE-writing for non-problem banks. The report often deals with complex issues that must be understood by the board. It must also be persuasive to encourage corrective action. The report will also provide the essential foundation for any enforcement action that may be required. Therefore, the amount of detail and the necessity for precise wording is especially important.

To ensure its clarity and effectiveness, the ROE should:

- Convey the information directors will need to understand the bank's problems, their relative severity, and effect on the bank if left uncorrected.

- Remain balanced, objective, and avoid a condescending tone or undue focus on personalities. The tone and findings in the ROE should be consistent with those presented during the exit meeting.

- Reflect the stage of the bank's rehabilitation process and management's competency/ability to correct noted deficiencies.

- Prioritize the issues and link the bank's problem to the underlying root cause and effect.

- Concentrate on the most crucial issues affecting the bank and critical steps toward improvement.

- Highlight uncorrected deficiencies from prior examinations or other areas needing corrective action.

- Provide an accurate assessment and description of the bank's conditions and management's responses and commitments for corrective action, including "who," "what," and "when."

- Contain sufficient documentation and information to support any informal or formal enforcement action, including receivership where appropriate.

E. Communicating Concerns to Other Regulators

Ongoing communication with other regulators is necessary to ensure the smooth resolution of a problem bank. Communicating concerns to other regulators should take place well before the resolution management stage, but will likely intensify as bank conditions worsen. In coordinating these communications, examiners must be aware of existing information-sharing agreements, delegation orders, interagency agreements, internal guidance, and laws governing information-sharing with other regulators, particularly for problem banks involved in nonbanking activities. Examiners should be particularly aware of the provisions in the Gramm-Leach-Bliley Act (GLBA), which address information-sharing and the limitations on direct examination of a functionally regulated entity. Requests for reports from functional regulators or functionally regulated entities and matters involving the examination of functionally regulated entities should be communicated immediately to the appropriate District or Large Bank Deputy Comptroller.

Additional information is contained in the "Resolution Management" section of this guide and in the "Examination Planning and Control" and "Bank Supervision Processes" booklets of the *Comptroller's Handbook*.

F. Communication Resources

Many resources are available that provide more specific guidance on communicating in difficult situations. The Continuing Education division can assist examiners in identifying specific educational media that cover topics, such as negotiating, dealing with difficult people, and communicating concerns to the board and management. For example, the OCC's Problem Bank School provides training on this specific issue.

Rehabilitation of Problem Banks

The rehabilitation process is based on the development of a specific and viable plan for corrective action for each troubled institution and subsequent monitoring to ensure adherence to the plan. At the conclusion of this stage of problem bank resolution, a bank normally returns to a safe and sound condition or advances to treatment as a resolution candidate.

I. Corrective Action Overview

A. Determining the Need for Corrective Action

The OCC's supervisory process attempts to identify problems early enough to enable remedial action that will prevent serious deterioration in a bank's condition. Accordingly, when problems are detected, examiners must determine their severity promptly as well as the timing and form of any needed corrective action. Some factors to consider include:

- *What types of problems has the bank had in the past?* If current problems are similar to past ones, the bank may not have corrected the root cause of the problem. Corrective action may be warranted.

- *Has the severity of problems progressed?* If the severity of problems is increasing, more vigorous corrective action is warranted.

- *Is the ownership and management team the same as in the past?* If the management team has not changed, examiners should consider the type of response given to previously identified problems. If a change has occurred, examiners must look at responsiveness to recent corrective action, if applicable.

- *Does the management team have a history of identifying problems within the bank or do outside parties usually surface them?* Management's ability to identify problems will influence the need for corrective action. If third parties routinely surface problems, management may need more guidance in the corrective action process. This is an important consideration in determining the type of corrective action to use.

- *Does the management team have the ability to fix the current problem?* If management lacks the necessary skills, they will need guidance in taking corrective action.

- *Has the bank been placed under an enforcement action before? If so, how long ago and for what?* The date and nature of a prior action may trigger the need for a new enforcement action to effect correction of current supervisory problems.

In essence, examiners should take more severe action if management has failed to comply with previous requests for corrective action. If management has a proven track record, a less severe action may be warranted, unless the problems are significant.

B. Assessing the Types of Corrective Action

The OCC's corrective action policy combines individual judgment with a framework to ensure consistency of application. This policy is set forth in PPM 5310-3 (REV), dated November 19, 1993 ("Corrective Action PPM") (See Appendix B). As of the publication of this guide, the OCC was considering certain limited changes and enhancements to the Corrective Action PPM. While these revisions are not yet final, discussions in this section will highlight the likely substantive changes to the Corrective Action PPM. Future updates to this guide will fully incorporate the final edits to the PPM.

The Corrective Action PPM provides guidance on the nature and types of corrective action available based on a bank's prompt corrective action (PCA) category, composite ratings, and risk profile. Potential corrective actions range from informal advice and moral suasion to formal enforcement actions, such as cease and desist orders, PCA directives, and safety and soundness orders.

The selection of specific corrective measures should be tailored to the institution and designed to correct identified deficiencies, improve its overall condition, and return the bank to a safe and sound condition as quickly as possible. Therefore, examiners should be familiar with the full range of OCC supervisory tools. Supervisory and enforcement actions fall within two broad categories: informal and formal. The latter is generally more severe and enforceable by law. The severity of action chosen should be based *primarily* on the bank's current condition with consideration given to the cooperation, responsiveness, and capability of the board and management. The table on the next page summarizes various types of informal and formal supervisory and enforcement actions.

Examples of Informal and Formal Supervisory and Enforcement Actions

Type of Corrective Action	Description of Action
Informal Actions:	
OCC-Required Board Resolution	Bank-generated document designed to address one or more specific concerns identified by the OCC. It is not a binding legal document.
Commitment Letter	Document signed by bank representatives, reflecting specific written commitments to take corrective action in response to concerns identified by the OCC. It is not a binding legal document.
Memorandum of Understanding	A bilateral document similar to more formal enforcement actions in form and content. It is not a binding legal document.
Corporate Leverage	An action by the OCC to withhold or condition approvals as part of the corporate approval process.
Formal Actions:	
Formal Written Agreements pursuant to 12 USC 1818	A bilateral document signed by the board and the OCC. Its provisions are set out in an article-by-article form to prescribe necessary corrective action. Violation of a formal agreement can provide the legal basis for more serious proceedings (*e.g.*, cease and desist).
Consent Order pursuant to 12 USC 1818	Similar in format to a Formal Agreement. May be enforced through application to an U.S. district court. A Cease and Desist Order is identical to a Consent Order but is imposed on an involuntary basis following an administrative hearing.

Type of Corrective Action	Description of Action
Temporary Cease and Desist Order Pursuant to 12 USC 1818	Interim order to impose immediate measures pending resolution of a final cease and desist order. May be challenged in U.S. district court within 10 days of issuance but effective on issuance.
Capital Directive pursuant to 12 CFR 3	An order designed for establishing and enforcing capital levels and for taking capital-related action. May be issued without a hearing before an administrative law judge.
Civil Money Penalties	Authorized civil money penalties for violations of law, formal written agreements, final orders, conditions imposed in writing, and certain unsafe and unsound banking practices and breach of fiduciary duty.
Conservatorship	Places the rights to control or dispose of the bank in the hands of an OCC-appointed conservator.
PCA Measures	Mandatory and discretionary measures based on a bank's PCA category (*e.g.*, restrictions)
Orders Enforcing Safety and Soundness Standards pursuant to 12 USC 1831p-1 12 CFR 30	Non-capital based supervisory restrictions for banks that fail to comply with established safety and soundness standards. Following agency notification of a deficiency, the bank may be directed to submit a compliance plan. If the bank fails to submit a timely, acceptable plan, or fails to adhere to an accepted plan, the OCC may issue an order requiring the bank to take corrective action.

The Corrective Action PPM provides flexibility in selecting a corrective action, while outlining presumptions for taking certain actions. Specifically, the policy states that the OCC will continue to rely primarily on informal and formal actions under 12 USC 1818, or other forms of non-PCA measures, to address supervisory concerns for banks that are "well-" or "adequately-" capitalized under the OCC's PCA regulations. For banks below the adequately capitalized level, the OCC will normally use PCA-based enforcement tools.

Informal Actions

Informal actions are commonly used in "well-" or "adequately-" capitalized banks, banks with composite ratings of 1- or 2-, and 3-rated banks with strong management. While this general rule continues, there are a number of potential changes to the Corrective Action PPM with respect to the use of informal actions. The most significant possible change is to narrow the types of informal actions used by the OCC by eliminating Board Resolutions as an approved form of action. In the interim, prior to the issuance of the revised Corrective Action PPM, examiners should consult with their supervisory office before using a Board Resolution.

For 1- or 2-rated banks, the Corrective Action PPM states that,

> Examiners and the supervisory office should obtain affirmative commitments for corrective action from the bank's senior management, the board of directors, and where appropriate, ownership. Such commitments need not take the form of an enforcement action if the examiner and the supervisory office consider other measures (*e.g.*, oral assurances, correspondence, or action taken or promised) adequate to address OCC criticisms.

Three-rated banks with strong management should be considered for informal action if other circumstances suggest that the remedial measures necessary to restore the bank to a safe and sound condition are present. In addition, the capability, cooperation, integrity, and commitment of the bank's management, board, and ownership are considerations in choosing the appropriate action.

Informal actions also are used to put the board and management on notice in case a formal action may be necessary later. They commonly provide more guidance and detail about deficiencies than that typically provided in a ROE. They also memorialize the board's commitments to correct problems.

Informal actions are unenforceable. This means that if the bank violates any articles or refuses to comply, the OCC cannot enforce compliance in federal court or assess civil money penalties (CMP) for noncompliance. Therefore, if an informal action does not result in the desired outcome, the OCC either has to persuade the bank through moral suasion or take a more severe formal action.

Formal Actions

A strong presumption exists to take formal action against all 4- and 5-rated banks. The OCC is considering possible changes to the Corrective Action PPM with respect to the use of formal actions. Under these revisions, if a 4-rated bank is subject only to an informal enforcement action, the supervisory office must consider imposing a formal enforcement action when the bank's rating is reaffirmed, or downgraded to a 5-rating. Potential changes to the PPM also would require the supervisory office to consider imposing a formal enforcement action against a 5-rated bank when the OCC has reaffirmed the rating. Any recommendation to maintain an informal action in such situations in lieu of a formal action must be supported by the appropriate Supervisory Review Committee (SRC).

Under the existing Corrective Action PPM and going forward, formal action or PCA should be considered for 3-rated banks with weak management or when conditions are deteriorating rapidly. The corrective measures should be appropriately severe and explicit as to implementation. As stated previously, the capability, cooperation, integrity, and commitment of the bank management, its board, and ownership are considerations in choosing the appropriate action.

Formal actions are appropriate when a bank has significant problems, especially when there is a threat of harm to the institution. Such actions are also used when corrective action by the board is not forthcoming, or when informal actions are insufficient. In some circumstances, there is a presumption for formal action, regardless of the bank's capital level and composite CAMELS rating. That presumption in favor of formal action exists when one or more of the following conditions exist:

- Significant problems in the bank's systems, controls, policies, internal audit programs, or MIS.
- Significant insider abuse or compliance problems.
- Failure to respond to prior supervisory efforts.
- Substantial noncompliance or lack of full compliance over an extended period of time. Revisions to the PPM would provide that any failure to achieve compliance with an informal enforcement action or with matters of concern contained in ROEs would establish a

presumption in favor of formal action.

Formal actions are authorized by statute. Because formal actions are enforceable, the OCC can assess CMPs against banks and individuals for noncompliance with a formal agreement, consent order, or a cease and desist order and can request a federal court to issue an injunction requiring the bank to comply with an order. Unlike informal actions, formal enforcement actions are public and are listed on the OCC's web site.

PCA Measures

As set forth at 12 USC 1831o and 12 CFR 6, PCA requires that the banking agencies take increasingly severe supervisory and enforcement actions as a bank's capital level diminishes. The OCC may reclassify a bank's capital category down one level if a bank is operating in an unsafe or unsound condition or is engaging in an unsafe or unsound practice. Such reclassification authorizes the OCC to use the PCA measures available for the lower capital level, subject to some limits.

For banks that are "undercapitalized," "significantly undercapitalized," or "critically undercapitalized" under Part 6 of the OCC's regulations, the Corrective Action PPM provides that the agency will consider using PCA measures in lieu of 12 USC 1818 enforcement actions.

Potential revisions to the Corrective Action PPM will make clear that when an undercapitalized, significantly undercapitalized, or critically undercapitalized bank is already subject to a formal enforcement action under 12 USC 1818, the OCC may elect to (1) keep the section 1818 document in place in its present form; (2) modify the document to reflect any additional requirements deemed necessary in light of the bank's capital category; (3) replace the document with a PCA directive if PCA is considered a more effective supervisory measure; or (4) impose a PCA directive while maintaining a formal enforcement action against the bank.

Whatever option the OCC chooses, additional mandatory PCA restrictions applicable to such banks will apply automatically. Additional information about PCA measures is discussed in the "Resolving Credit and Capital Impairment Problems" section of this guide.

Safety and Soundness Standards

The OCC also has the authority under 12 USC 1831p-1 and 12 CFR 30 to issue a safety and soundness order against a bank that fails to meet established safety and soundness standards. Operational and managerial standards have been established under Part 30 in the following areas:

- Internal controls and information systems.
- Internal audit system.
- Loan documentation.
- Credit underwriting.
- Interest rate exposure.
- Asset growth.
- Asset quality.

- Earnings.
- Compensation fees and benefits.

This tool was designed to address unsafe and unsound conduct that is not reflected in bank capital levels. Accordingly, Part 30 orders generally are used to address specific problems in "well-" or "adequately-" capitalized banks. The Corrective Action PPM provides that such actions should be taken only if the deficiency is not already the subject of an enforcement action, and the bank is at least adequately capitalized for PCA purposes.

Pursuant to statute and Part 30, a bank that fails to comply with any of the above safety and soundness standards must file a plan with the OCC to correct the deficiency. If a bank fails to file a required plan or fails to implement satisfactorily a plan approved by the OCC, the OCC must, by order, require the bank to correct the deficiency. The OCC also has the discretion to require the bank, by order, to take any other action that the OCC determines will better carry its statutory mandate. The OCC is required to take additional action against a bank that fails to submit or implement an acceptable plan if the bank has also undergone either extraordinary growth[10] or a change in control (see 12 CFR 30.4 (d)).

Other Formal Actions

OCC policy provides that the examiner or supervisory office will consider CMP assessments or more severe actions in cases of substantial noncompliance with a formal enforcement document.

In some cases, the OCC has the authority to place a bank into receivership or conservatorship, even if the institution is liquid and meets the applicable capital requirements. However, these measures are used only in the most severe cases, such as a bank riddled with insider abuse with no realistic possibility for rehabilitation, a bank with significant unsafe and unsound practices that have had a substantial negative effect on the bank, a bank that has concealed its records from the OCC, or a bank that has another of the material failings listed in the receivership provisions. This is discussed in the "Grounds for Receivership and Early Resolution" section of "Resolution Management."

C. The Corrective Action Process

To ensure consistency, while preserving the flexibility to fashion the most appropriate form(s) of corrective action in response to specific circumstances, the OCC has developed a formal process to review proposed corrective actions. An important part of that process is the Washington and district SRCs. Under the Corrective Action PPM, the appropriate SRC makes recommendations for decisions on all formal enforcement actions; any decisions to modify, terminate, or reduce the severity of existing enforcement actions, and the content of any new enforcement actions on all 3-, 4-, or 5-rated banks; any exceptions to policy; and any actions involving use of OCC's PCA authority or safety and soundness orders. The relevant SRC assesses all proposed corrective actions in conjunction with the OCC's supervisory strategy for the bank and OCC policy.

---

[10]   For this purpose, extraordinary growth means an increase in assets of more that 7.5 percent during any quarter within the 18-month period preceding the request for a compliance plan (12 CFR 30.4 (d)(2)).

The timeliness of corrective action is critical. Corrective action should be taken as soon as practical once an examiner or supervisory office has identified and documented a need for such action. When circumstances warrant, the supervisory office may take appropriate action during an examination. Otherwise, the supervisory office must recommend whether to initiate corrective action, or to change (upgrade or downgrade) an existing corrective action, within 15 calendar days of the following decisions or determinations:

- A final decision to assign or retain a 3-, 4-, or 5-rated bank's composite rating.
- A decision to downgrade any bank's rating to a 3, 4, or 5.
- A determination that a bank is significantly or critically undercapitalized.
- A determination that an undercapitalized bank has failed to submit an acceptable capital plan or has failed in some material respect to implement it.
- A determination that a bank has violated a safety and soundness standard.

Corrective Action Documents

The examiner and the supervisory office must document in writing decisions on whether to proceed with an enforcement action or PCA directive and the nature and severity of the action. These decisions should be recorded in the OCC's electronic information system.

Within 15 days following the final SRC decision, the supervisory office must provide to the bank's board of directors, or its duly authorized representative, a copy of the proposed enforcement document. The supervisory office must also arrange for a meeting with the board of directors to present the document and obtain its execution, if applicable. This meeting should normally occur within 30 days of the final SRC decision.

Corrective action documents should address substantive supervisory problems. Although it is not necessary to address every supervisory issue identified, all documents should clearly list any prohibited or restricted activities, prioritize remedial measures to be taken, and the time in which the bank, its board or directors or management must act. Although the language in corrective action documents may be similar to existing documents, the supervisory office should tailor specific remedial action for each individual bank. Although not mandatory, virtually every enforcement action addressing safety and soundness issues has an article requiring a minimum capital level, as capital is the key determinant in many supervisory decisions affecting the bank.

The final corrective action document must:

- Be enforceable.
- Specify measurable corrective actions for determining compliance.
- Be linked to the supervisory issues and root causes identified in the ROE.
- Establish reasonable time frames for performance.

After SRC has decided that an enforcement action is appropriate, the examiner must guide bank management through the process. If management and the board know what to expect, they should be more easily persuaded of the benefits of agreeing or consenting to the document. The EIC should explain that management, the board, and legal counsel will be able to review the draft document. By providing advance copies of enforcement actions, the OCC hopes to negotiate and resolve outstanding issues so that the document can be executed at a board meeting. The draft enforcement action is subject to changes in content through the negotiation process. An OCC representative is designated to negotiate changes with the bank prior to this process.

The board meeting should focus on issues requiring the board's attention and the corrective action plan — the enforcement action. The board meeting is not the forum to negotiate documents. During this meeting, the examiner should stress that the board and the OCC have the same goals for the bank (*e.g.*, a profitable, well-managed bank that engages in safe and sound operations). The enforcement action is merely a blueprint for the board to help meet those goals.

Sometimes a board refuses to sign an enforcement action at the board meeting. The OCC may or may not have an indication that signing will occur at the meeting. Usually, an OCC attorney will attend the board meeting when an enforcement action is presented for signature. The attorney will answer any legal questions and explain the enforcement action process. If the board will not sign the enforcement action, the attorney will serve a "Notice of Charges." This notice alleges unsafe and unsound practices and violations of law and regulation identified in the examination report that correspond to the articles proposed in the enforcement action. Serving the Notice of Charges also starts the administrative hearing process. Even after the Notice is served, the bank can settle anytime by electing to execute the proposed document. The vast majority of all administrative enforcement actions are resolved through negotiated settlement.

Follow-up Actions

Once an enforcement action is signed, the bank must still successfully implement the corrective action plan. This often requires a significant change in the behavior of directors, officers, and employees throughout the institution, and such changes are not always easy. Examiners can facilitate the process of change by following up closely on how well the bank is implementing its corrective action plan and providing constructive advice on where the bank is falling short of OCC's expectations.

Given that improvement in a bank's condition is associated with the timely achievement of compliance with an enforcement action, examiners should communicate with the bank both orally and in writing on a regular basis regarding its compliance efforts. The Corrective Action PPM requires an on-site follow-up of compliance with new enforcement actions within 60 days of the latest due date in the enforcement action. During this on-site follow up, examiners should provide advice to bankers in developing the rehabilitation programs required by the enforcement action. For those programs in place, examiners should test transactions for compliance with the new programs. Examiners should also meet with senior management and directors to answer any questions about the requirements of the document and to explain what the bank must do to achieve compliance.

A significant focus of the potential revisions to the Corrective Action PPM concerns the OCC's assessment of the bank's compliance with outstanding enforcement documents, especially with respect to banks that are not in "full" compliance with all articles in those documents. Under revisions to the Corrective Action PPM presently under consideration, a bank will be considered in compliance with an enforcement article only if it has adopted, implemented, and adhered to all of the corrective actions set forth in the article, and OCC examiners have verified through the examination process that the bank has done so.

A bank should not be considered in compliance with an article in an enforcement document merely because they have made progress or a good faith effort towards complying with the article. There is a strong presumption to take more severe action if, based on the results of an on-site assessment or subsequent assessment, the bank is found to be in noncompliance with the document. However, the supervisory office may, in its discretion, grant reasonable extensions of time to comply with articles that require the development and implementation of policies, procedures, systems, and controls.

Following the on-site follow up, examiners must communicate the OCC's assessment of the bank's compliance efforts in writing (usually a letter to the board of directors). The potential revisions to the Corrective Action PPM will provide specific guidance on examiner actions with respect to articles with which there is less than "full" compliance. Until those revisions are finalized, examiner communications must specifically detail what the bank must do to achieve compliance for those articles in "partial compliance" or "noncompliance."

Results of the follow up visit should then be incorporated into the supervisory strategy and work plans for the bank. For example, based on the severity of the bank's problems and early compliance efforts, a second follow-up on-site may be necessary. At the next full scope examination of the bank, examiners should assess whether:

- The enforcement action had its intended effect.
- The provisions in the enforcement action remain appropriate for the bank's situation. If not, should the enforcement action be amended, terminated, or replaced by another document?

The potential revisions to the Corrective Action PPM will also establish additional follow-up requirements on outstanding enforcement actions. Specifically, these revisions will require the appropriate SRC to assess the bank's compliance with outstanding enforcement documents within six months of the effective date of the action and after every on-site review.

An action generally should not be terminated until the bank has complied with all articles in the document. Recommendations to change or terminate any actions on 3-, 4-, or 5-rated banks, and any formal actions, must be approved by the supervisory office and SRC.

Community Bank Case — Taking Appropriate Corrective Action

A good, if somewhat unusual, example of appropriate corrective action occurred in the supervision of a small community bank. The bank had an extremely factious board of directors. The infighting among board members was so severe that the two factions had filed numerous lawsuits against each other and were not communicating. Consequently, board meetings were not held, and even routine business matters languished. Examiners' efforts to obtain voluntary corrective action to address deficiencies were unsuccessful. Although the bank's condition was not yet seriously affected, it was evident that, unless the stalemate was broken, the bank's condition would decline.

The EIC, together with the supervisory office, Special Supervision/Fraud, district legal and Enforcement and Compliance devised a strategy to address the situation. Finding that the bank had failed to comply with the Part 30 Safety and Soundness Standards, the OCC notified the bank of the deficiency and gave it a short time period to submit a compliance plan. When the bank failed to do so, the OCC issued a notice of intent to issue a safety and soundness order. The bank failed to submit a persuasive response. Thus, the OCC imposed an order requiring the bank to appoint a new director immediately to break the deadlock. After determining that the bank would not comply, the supervisory office advised the board in writing that the agency planned to begin assessing civil money penalties at the rate of $5M per day against each director personally until the bank complied with the order. Almost immediately, the board appointed a new director, and the deadlock was broken. Shortly thereafter, the supervisory office removed the order. Today the bank is healthy and operating in a safe and sound manner.

This case illustrates all of the elements of effective problem bank supervision. The examiners identified the problem early, brought it to the board's attention, and attempted to obtain a commitment to take corrective action. They monitored the bank's progress closely and when it became apparent that voluntary corrective action would not be forthcoming, the agency took increasingly severe supervisory and enforcement actions, until the problem was resolved.

II. Resolving Credit and Capital Impairment Problems

Capital can dissipate rapidly in the face of significant credit losses, underscoring the importance of early detection and timely resolution of supervisory concerns.

A. Reviewing Credit Risk

Despite the evolution of the banking system and the introduction of new products and services, lending activities remain the predominant source of income and financial risk to banks. Off-balance-sheet activities, such as derivatives and securitizations, are sources of additional credit risk. Moreover, OCC studies have shown that commercial underwriting standards have been steadily declining in recent years, and that inherent credit risk in the system is building. As loan structures become more liberal, the potential for loss in the event of default escalates. This structural weakness in loan underwriting has profound and far-reaching implications for the banking system in an economic downturn. Therefore, examiners must determine the true level of existing and potential credit risk in a problem bank to develop realistic and appropriate supervisory plans and remedies.

Problem loans are classified based on the examiner's best judgment of probability of default and the likelihood of orderly liquidation. Because no formula covers all types of loans made by banks, loan review and classification require mature credit judgment and a basic understanding of the following interagency policy definitions:

- *Special Mention* — Loans that have potential weaknesses that deserve management's close attention. If left uncorrected, these potential weaknesses may result in deterioration of the repayment prospects for the loan or in the institution's credit position at some future date. Special Mention loans are not adversely classified and do not expose an institution to sufficient risk to warrant adverse classification.

- *Substandard* — Loans that are inadequately protected by the current sound worth and paying capacity of the obligor or by any collateral pledged. Loans so classified must have a well-defined weakness or weaknesses that jeopardize the liquidation of the debt and are characterized by the distinct possibility that the bank will sustain some loss if the deficiencies are not corrected.

- *Doubtful* — Loans that have all the weaknesses inherent in those classified as substandard, with the added characteristic that existing facts, conditions, and values make collection or liquidation in full highly improbable. The possibility of loss is extremely high, but because of certain important and reasonably specific pending factors that may work to the advantage and strengthening of the asset, its classification as an estimated loss is deferred until a more exact status may be determined. Pending factors include merger, acquisition, liquidation procedures, capital injection, additional collateral, new financing sources, or additional guarantors.

- *Loss* — Loans that are considered uncollectible and of such little value that its continuance as bankable assets is not warranted. This classification does not mean that the loan has absolutely no recovery or salvage value. Rather, the amount of loss is difficult to measure and it is not practical or desirable to defer writing off this basically worthless asset even though partial recovery may be obtained in the future. Loans should be charged off in the period in which they are deemed uncollectible.

Additional information relating to problem loan classification, review, and accounting can be found in section 215.1 of the *Comptroller's Handbook for National Bank Examiners,* the "Loan Portfolio Management" booklet of the *Comptroller's Handbook,* and the "Accounting Issues in Problem Banks" section of this document.

As part of their credit review, examiners must also ensure that banks have an adequate allowance for loan and lease losses (ALLL). The ALLL is a valuation reserve established and maintained by charges against the bank's operating income. As a valuation reserve, it is an estimate of uncollectible amounts that is used to reduce the book value of loans and leases to the amount that is expected to be collected. The ALLL must be maintained at a level adequate to address estimated inherent losses in the loan portfolio as of the evaluation date. For additional information on the ALLL, see the "Allowance for Loan and Lease Losses" booklet of the *Comptroller's Handbook.*

B. Managing Capital

Various banking laws and regulations mandate minimum capital levels for banks and detail actions for both the bank and supervisors if capital falls below those established minimums. The statutory requirements are minimums, and the OCC has the authority to require more capital in banks with significant risk. The OCC may also limit or prohibit dividends under certain circumstances.

Managing the Capital Needed to Meet Statutory Requirements

The bank capital requirements contained in PCA (12 USC 1830o and 12 CFR 6) and 12 CFR 3 specify various minimum ratios of capital to assets that banks must maintain. Both PCA and Part 3 focus on both a leverage ratio and a risk-based capital ratio in establishing regulatory restrictions. The leverage ratio is based on total bank assets, while the risk-based capital ratios incorporate the riskiness of a bank's assets as defined under 12 CFR 3. The risk-based capital ratios are calculated by dividing total and Tier 1 capital by risk-weighted assets. A bank's on- and off-balance-sheet assets are assigned risk weights as described in 12 CFR 3, Appendix A.

A bank could take steps to improve its capital ratios by decreasing either total assets or the aggregate risk weight of its assets. However, in some cases those actions may only temporarily address the capital problems at the bank and, in the long term, may increase the overall risk to earnings and capital. Examiners should review carefully any actual or planned balance sheet changes to ensure that they address the capital issues at the bank effectively. Examiners should be wary of any changes to the balance sheet that improve a bank's capital position in the short-term, but are not part of a plan that adequately considers the bank's future financial condition.

To improve its leverage ratio, a bank could reduce total on-balance-sheet assets. There are many ways for a bank to accomplish this goal. The most obvious method is to sell assets directly. Another widely used method is securitization of bank assets. This is an activity that increasingly warrants examiner attention. If not used properly or managed effectively, asset securitization may actually increase risk to the bank. (For additional information, see the "Significant Off-Balance-Sheet Exposure" discussion in the Problem Bank Identification section) A third option for banks to reduce assets is to replace investment securities used to manage interest rate risk with off-balance-sheet interest rate swaps. A bank may be able to use swaps to effectively manage interest rate risk without increasing its balance sheet and capital requirements; however, care should be taken to ensure that bank management understands and is competent to engage in swap transactions before doing so.

Some asset reduction techniques may improve a bank's leverage ratio, but actually increase the risk to the bank. For example, a bank could reduce assets and increase capital by selling appreciated or low risk assets. A gain on the sale of assets increases net income that adds capital, and combined with the decrease in assets, improves the bank's leverage ratio. However, the risk to the bank has increased because it is left with proportionately more assets that are probably depreciated, less liquid, and riskier. The net result of this transaction is merely to increase risk and jeopardize future earnings and capital adequacy.

Another technique banks use to decrease assets and reduce capital requirements is a sale/leaseback arrangement for bank premises. A bank could sell the real estate with an agreement to lease the property back from the purchaser. Under this scenario, the bank has reduced its asset base and, therefore, its capital requirements, but may not have significantly improved the level of risk.

To improve its risk-based capital ratio, a bank could restructure its balance sheet and replace assets that require higher risk weights with lower risk-weighted assets. For example, a bank could sell loans or reduce loan volume, and invest in U.S. government securities. However, such balance sheet restructuring does not guarantee the long-term survival of the bank. Low risk assets generally earn a lower return, and the bank may face future earnings pressure and capital inadequacy that could lead to failure.

Retaining Capital

A bank that has insufficient capital should take steps to prevent further depletion. Paying dividends or repaying certain capital issuances could deplete a bank's capital base to an inadequate level and may constitute an unsafe and unsound banking practice, even though the failure to make such payments could have adverse market ramifications by signaling problems at the bank or parent holding company. When considering dividends and debt retirement, a problem bank's board of directors should use caution not to materially exacerbate any deficiency in the bank's capital. To ensure that this does not happen, the OCC has statutory and regulatory authority to restrict capital outflows in certain circumstances.

Dividends

All dividends must conform to the statutory requirements of 12 USC 56 and 60. Under 12 USC 56, a national bank may not pay a cash or property dividend[11] on its common stock if the dividend would exceed net undivided profits then on hand. In calculating available capital for 12 USC 56 purposes, a national bank cannot add its ALLL to undivided profits. Net undivided profits are the contribution to capital from a bank's past earnings. If a bank has experienced significant losses that equals or exceeds its past earnings or net undivided profits, it cannot pay a dividend, because the dividend would distribute the original capital investment in the bank.

Under 12 USC 60, a national bank must obtain prior approval from the OCC to pay cash dividends on either common or preferred stock that would exceed its net profits for the current year[12] combined with retained net profits[13] of the prior two years. This requirement to seek prior approval for a dividend does not prohibit a bank from paying dividends. Rather, it enables the OCC to review the bank's status and future prospects to determine whether payment of the proposed dividend would result in an unsafe or unsound condition detrimental to the bank's best interests. The OCC's prior approval process for dividends is described in Appendix C.

---

[11]   A property dividend is a distribution to shareholders in a form other than cash, including distributions of stock and real or personal property of the bank. A property dividend requires prior OCC approval. Stock dividends are subject to 12 USC 56, but not 12 USC 60.

[12]   The term net profits is defined as net income as reported in the bank's Consolidated Reports of Condition and Income with no adjustments.

[13]   The term retained net profits is defined as net profits minus dividends paid.

There are situations in which a national bank should not pay a dividend, even if such a payment complies with the provisions of 12 USC 56 and 60. For example, paying dividends that deplete a bank's capital base to an inadequate level constitutes an unsafe and unsound banking practice. At other times, the directors may decide not to issue a dividend, because they wish to preserve capital to support future growth or to provide protection against unexpected losses.

In addition to the regulatory and legal restrictions, examiners may prevent the outflow of capital from a bank through the use of supervisory actions. Any enforcement action that requires a national bank to raise additional capital, or to maintain a certain level of capital, should require the bank to obtain prior approval from the OCC before paying a dividend. If prior approval will not be required, the supervisory office should document in the OCC's electronic database the justification for this decision. PCA also places limits on dividends and other capital distributions. As discussed more fully in the "Prompt Corrective Action" section that follows, banks cannot pay a cash or property dividend, if such payment results in the bank falling into the undercapitalized category.

In some cases, a bank may make a payment that constitutes a dividend, even though the bank does not label it as such. In one case, for example, a national bank paid its parent holding company for a *pro rata* portion of the holding company directors' fees. Through the management fees, the directors of the national bank received compensation from the bank for their duties and responsibilities. All bank directors also served as directors of the holding company and received additional compensation from it for separate holding company duties. Since the duties of the holding company directors did not provide a direct benefit to the bank, the OCC examiners determined that the bank should not reimburse the holding company for a *pro rata* portion of the directors' fees. The payment to the holding company, therefore, constituted a dividend. Additionally, the national bank did not have net profits available to pay dividends; net profits (loss) were ($900M). Since net profits were insufficient to support a dividend payment, the bank was required to seek OCC approval prior to paying the dividend. The national bank did not seek prior approval. The OCC examiners identified the illegal payment during an examination and informed the bank of its violation of 12 USC 60 and 12 CFR 5.64. The bank requested and obtained reimbursement from the holding company for the payments.

Restrictions on Repayments

OCC regulations restrict the repayment of certain instruments that qualify as capital under limited circumstances. For example, the OCC's risk-based capital standards permit the use of hybrid instruments[14] that meet certain criteria as supplementary or Tier 2 capital. To qualify as Tier 2 capital, a hybrid instrument's documentation must specify that prior OCC approval is required for redemption prior to maturity. Additionally, the instrument must also provide for an option to defer principal and interest payments if the bank had no net profit for the most recent four quarters and eliminated dividends on common and preferred stock. The other criteria for Tier 2 qualification are outlined in Appendix A of 12 CFR 3.[15]

---

[14]   Hybrid instruments have characteristics of both debt and equity.

[15]   Repayment restrictions also apply to the use of Tier 3 capital instruments. See Appendix B of 12 CFR 3.

Payments on subordinated debt are restricted by OCC capital regulations as well as by PCA. Under 12 CFR 3.100(f), no prepayments on subordinated debt are permitted without prior OCC approval unless the bank remains an "eligible" bank after the prepayment. An eligible bank is well-capitalized and has a CAMELS composite rating of 1 or 2. Additionally, PCA prohibits critically undercapitalized banks from making any payments of principal or interest on the bank's subordinated debt (without prior approval) beginning 60 days after becoming critically undercapitalized.

Raising Additional Capital

Although not always possible in seriously troubled cases, the most direct way for a problem bank to improve its ratios and reduce risk is by raising additional capital. This can be attempted privately through the bank's holding company, directors, or other shareholders, or publicly by accessing the capital markets. The most common form of new capital for banks results from the downstreaming of proceeds from a securities issuance at the parent holding company level. However, a company experiencing significant financial difficulties will have trouble obtaining capital at reasonable rates because investors naturally are reluctant to invest in risky or poorly performing companies.

A bank's board of directors must consider many issues in its decision to obtain new capital. In some cases, banks, and not parent holding companies, are subject to securities registration requirements. For example, a registered national bank with more than 500 shareholders must register the securities and file certain periodic reports with the OCC under 12 CFR 11. Those reports include quarterly and annual financial reports to shareholders and proxy statements for shareholder meetings. A bank with less than 500 shareholders is exempt from those requirements. A bank with less than 500 shareholders must consider the additional cost and burden of complying with those requirements when contemplating a stock offering to raise capital that might increase the total number of shareholders to more than 500.

If a privately owned bank decides to "go public" and raise equity capital by selling stock that will be traded on a stock exchange, the bank must comply with 12 CFR 16, which covers securities offering disclosure rules, and with 12 CFR 11. Raising capital in the capital markets, particularly for a private bank that wishes to become public, requires significant management time and effort and can be costly. As outlined in 12 CFR 16, the OCC requires a detailed registration statement and prospectus for the sale of securities to the public. Before a bank can raise capital by selling securities, the OCC must declare the prospectus effective. A significant marketing effort usually is necessary to inform investors about the bank and induce them to invest. Such a marketing effort, often called a "road show," requires senior management participation. Additionally, bank management should recognize that issuing new securities will dilute the ownership interest of existing shareholders and may depress a company's stock price. In fact, many investors interpret the offering of new shares as an indicator of financial problems.

Capital Plans under 12 CFR 3

A bank experiencing problems should recognize the need to raise additional capital before it falls to the undercapitalized level, as defined in PCA, or its risk-based capital ratios fall below the regulatory minimums. If a bank does not undertake a capital raising effort independently, the OCC may legally require the bank to develop and implement a plan to increase capital.

The OCC historically has required banks that do not meet the regulatory capital minimums to submit capital plans as described in 12 CFR 3.7. The availability of PCA authority, however, has made use of 12 CFR 3.7 much more infrequent. In some cases, the OCC may determine that, because of the nature of the bank's activities, risk exposure, or financial condition, risk-based capital ratios that exceed the minimums in 12 CFR 3 are necessary. Such banks also would be required to submit capital plans under 12 CFR 3.7 if their capital falls below the required amount. Under 12 CFR 3.7, a capital plan should describe how the bank will meet the minimum capital ratios (*e.g.,* increase capital via a public offering, slow loan growth, sell assets) and present the timetable for the planned actions. Examiners should review the plan to determine whether the bank's planned actions are realistic and address identified problems.

The OCC can require a bank to develop a capital plan under 12 CFR 3.7 before it becomes undercapitalized according to PCA. Unlike the requirements under PCA, which focus solely on the amount of capital, the minimum capital ratios of 12 CFR 3 are based on the bank's risk profile. The OCC encourages a capital plan, prepared under 12 CFR 3.7, to be reasonably consistent with Capital Restoration Plan (CRP) requirements under PCA to avoid duplicating efforts, should the bank become undercapitalized. However, a capital plan submitted under Part 3 is not acceptable as a CRP under PCA, unless the statutory requirements of 12 USC 1831o(e), described below, are addressed.

C. Prompt Corrective Action

Examiners must be aware of the requirements imposed by statute for the supervision of problem banks. For banks facing emerging and excessive risks to capital, the requirements of PCA are now essential to the problem bank rehabilitation process. PCA includes provisions for discretionary and mandatory supervisory actions, and examiners should be familiar with both.

The statutory and regulatory framework of PCA established a capital-based supervisory scheme that requires regulators to place increasingly stringent restrictions on banks as regulatory capital levels decline. Capital levels under PCA are similar to, but distinct from, capital adequacy principles under 12 CFR 3. Although 12 CFR 3 specifies minimum capital requirements consistent with a bank's risk profile, that minimum may not accurately reflect the level of capital actually necessary to support the bank's operations. Similarly, a bank in the well-capitalized category of PCA may have inadequate capital for the purposes of Part 3. PCA merely assigns banks to certain capital categories and subjects them to the respective requirements, limitations, and restrictions of those categories. Regardless of a bank's capital level, no bank is considered "well-capitalized" under PCA if it is subject to a cease and desist order, a formal agreement, or a capital or PCA directive that requires the bank to achieve or maintain a higher level of capital.

The following are the Prompt Corrective Action capital categories:

Capital Category	Total RBC	Tier 1 RBC	Tier 1 Leverage
Well-Capitalized	$\geq 10\%$	$\geq 6\%$	$\geq 5\%$
Adequately Capitalized	$\geq 8\%$	$\geq 4\%*$	$\geq 4\%$
Undercapitalized	$< 8\%$	$< 4\%*$	$< 4\%$
Significantly Undercapitalized	$< 6\%$	$< 3\%$	$< 3\%$

* Three percent for 1-rated banks

Critically Undercapitalized: Tangible Equity $\leq 2\%$
The tangible equity ratio is defined as tier 1 capital PLUS cumulative preferred stock and related surplus LESS intangibles, except qualifying purchased mortgage servicing rights (PMSR) divided by total assets LESS intangibles, except qualifying PMSR.

PCA contains an important provision that authorizes examiners to reclassify a bank's capital category to the next lower level when based on supervisory criteria per 12 USC 1831o(g). This discretionary aspect of PCA is used when examiners determine that a bank is in an unsafe or unsound condition or is engaging in an unsafe or unsound practice. For example, if the bank is well-capitalized, the OCC can reclassify it to the "adequately capitalized" category. Likewise, if the bank is in the "adequately capitalized" category, OCC can reclassify it to "undercapitalized." Once reclassified, the bank may be subject to one or more limitations, requirements, and restrictions applicable to that category under PCA. Written notice is provided to the bank of the OCC's intent to reclassify the bank's PCA category. The bank may request an informal hearing, to be presided over by an OCC official not involved in the initial recommendation, to reclassify the bank.

The OCC may also apply corrective measures to undercapitalized or significantly undercapitalized banks that normally are only available for banks in the next lower PCA category. To make use of this authority, the OCC must determine that such measures are necessary to carry out the purposes of 12 USC 1831o.

PCA Restrictions

Restrictions for All Banks

All banks, regardless of their capital level, are prohibited from making any capital distribution or paying a management fee to any person who controls the bank, if after making the distribution or paying the fee, the bank would be undercapitalized. Banks that operate with capital levels near the regulatory minimum must ensure that dividends will not cause the bank to violate those restrictions.

Restrictions for Adequately Capitalized Banks

An adequately capitalized bank must apply for and receive a waiver from the FDIC before it can accept, renew or rollover brokered deposits. Until such waiver is received, the bank may not use a broker, and the bank is limited to paying rates of deposits to no more than 75 basis points over the average rate of local financial institutions. A national rate cannot be used unless a waiver is received. This topic is discussed fully in the "Resolving Liquidity Problems" section.

Restrictions for Undercapitalized Banks

When a bank becomes undercapitalized, it is subject to several mandatory requirements, imposed by law without any action by the OCC. Those mandatory measures applicable to undercapitalized banks are:

- Submission of a Capital Restoration Plan (CRP), with resultant close monitoring by the supervisory office.
- Absent an approved CRP and specific OCC findings, restrictions on asset growth.
- Absent an approved CRP and specific OCC findings, restrictions on certain expansion of activities, including acquisitions, new branches and new lines of businesses.

If necessary to carry out the purposes of PCA, the OCC may impose on undercapitalized banks any of the restrictions applicable to significantly undercapitalized banks. Those restrictions are discussed below.

One of the most significant mandates for an undercapitalized bank is the requirement to file an acceptable CRP. The CRP is one of the most important documents in the rehabilitation of problem banks and must be filed by the bank within 45 days of notification of undercapitalized status. An acceptable CRP should set forth the most efficient and expeditious way for that bank, in light of its current conditions and future prospects, to return to an adequately capitalized status. The CRP also may be important in later resolution of the bank if the bank does not improve. An undercapitalized bank's failure to submit or implement a CRP can be grounds for appointment of a receiver.

To prepare an acceptable CRP, a bank's board of directors and management must analyze its current condition and future prospects to determine the most expedient way to return it to the adequately capitalized category. Elements of the CRP should include current and pro-forma balance sheets, current and long-term budgets, a strategic plan for the bank, the market analysis used to derive the appropriate means to raise capital, and any other relevant information. The CRP should detail clearly the assumptions used in the analysis.

The CRP must address:

- The steps the bank will take to become adequately capitalized.

- The levels of capital to be attained during each quarter of each year of the plan.
- The types and levels of activities in which the bank will engage.
- How management will comply with the restrictions against asset growth (see 12 USC 1831o(e)(3)) and acquisitions, branching, and new lines of business (see 12 USC 1831o(e)(4)).
- Any other information the OCC may require.

The OCC will not accept a CRP unless the plan contains the information required by statute, is based on realistic assumptions, is likely to succeed in restoring the bank's capital, and will not increase the risk to the bank. In addition, the OCC will not accept a CRP, unless each company controlling the bank submits a **written** guarantee of the plan. The guarantee ensures that the holding company will provide a financial commitment. In some cases the company controlling the bank may not be in a position to provide demonstrable financial support. Nonetheless, the guarantee must provide appropriate assurances of performance to the OCC that the company's subsidiary bank will comply with the CRP.

The guarantee should furnish, at a minimum, the holding company's financial commitment guaranteeing the bank's compliance with the CRP. In addition, the guarantee may include assurances that the company will:

- Take actions required by the CRP.
- Ensure the selection of competent management.
- Restrict transactions between the bank and the company.
- Discontinue certain risky or inappropriate bank or affiliate activities.

Depending on the company involved, the guarantee may also include "appropriate assurances of performance," such as a promissory note, a pledge of holding company assets, appropriate assurances from bank holding company counsel, a holding company board of directors' resolution, or other supervisory actions deemed necessary to ensure performance. More detailed information on the guarantee and a sample guarantee is contained in Appendix D and Appendix E, respectively. Additional discussion of guarantees is contained in the "Problems in Large and Multi-Charter Banking Companies" section later in this guide.

The OCC will notify the bank in writing of the CRP's acceptability within 60 days of receipt or must notify the bank in writing of any delay and the reason for the delay. The OCC supervisory office must submit a copy of each approved CRP to the FDIC's regional office within 45 days of approval. An undercapitalized bank that fails to submit or implement, in any material respect, an acceptable CRP is subject to the same restrictions that apply to significantly undercapitalized banks.

For undercapitalized banks that have failed to submit or implement an acceptable CRP, the OCC will do the following: restrict affiliate transactions, restrict interest rates paid on deposits, or require recapitalization. The statute also grants the OCC latitude to impose additional requirements normally imposed upon significantly undercapitalized banks. Such requirements may include:

- Electing a new board of directors by the shareholders.
- Hiring qualified senior executive officers subject to OCC approval.
- Dismissing directors or senior executive officers that held office for more than 180 days immediately before the institution became undercapitalized.
- Taking other appropriate action.

The dismissal of directors and senior executive officers under PCA does not constitute a 12 USC 1818 removal action. A removal under 12 USC 1818 is a permanent ban from banking and from all federally regulated institutions. A dismissal under PCA is specific to the position at that bank. The affected person may appeal the dismissal, but may not retain his/her position during the appeal and review period. The burden of proof is on the person to support reinstatement. The dismissed person must show that his/her continued employment in the position would strengthen materially the bank's ability to become adequately capitalized and to correct the unsafe or unsound condition or practice. All PCA directives or dismissals must go through WSRC.

Restrictions for Significantly Undercapitalized Banks

If the bank's capital falls to the significantly undercapitalized category, a new PCA notification letter is sent. Significantly undercapitalized banks are subject to the restrictions applicable to undercapitalized banks, including the requirement to submit an acceptable CRP. However, the bank does not have to file a revised CRP, unless required to do so in writing by the OCC. This requirement should be included in the notification letter. Also, the bank is subject to more demanding mandatory, presumptive and discretionary restrictions than those imposed on the undercapitalized institutions previously mentioned.

PCA requirements for significantly undercapitalized banks or undercapitalized banks that fail to submit or implement an acceptable CRP are described below.

Mandatory and/or Presumptive Measures:

- OCC approval before paying any bonus or increasing compensation to a senior executive officer. If the bank has not submitted an acceptable CRP, the OCC may not approve such a request.
- Requiring recapitalization.
- Restrictions on transactions with affiliates.
- Restrictions on interest rates and the use of brokered deposits.

Discretionary Measures:

- Requiring sale of voting shares.
- Further restrictions on asset growth. PCA may also require a reduction in total assets.
- Restriction on activities. PCA may require that the bank or subsidiaries reduce or eliminate any activity the OCC determines will result in excessive risk.
- New election of the board.
- Dismissal of directors and officers. These include directors or senior executive officers that

held office for more than 180 days immediately before the bank became undercapitalized.
- New senior executive officers. PCA may require the bank to hire qualified senior executive officers subject to OCC approval.
- Prohibition of deposits from correspondent banks.
- The divestiture of subsidiaries. PCA may require the divestiture of any subsidiary that is in danger of becoming insolvent and cause a significant risk to the bank or is likely to significantly affect the bank's assets or earnings.
- Other action that the OCC determines will better resolve the bank's problems at the least possible long-term cost to the deposit insurance fund.

PCA provisions for significantly undercapitalized banks or undercapitalized banks that fail to submit or implement an acceptable CRP also authorize the OCC to take action leading to the resolution of the bank:

- Requiring the bank to be sold or to merge into another bank, if certain other requirements are present.
- Appointing a receiver for the bank.

Restrictions for Critically Undercapitalized Banks

Critically undercapitalized banks are subject to all restrictions applicable to undercapitalized and significantly undercapitalized banks. In addition, when a bank's ratio of tangible equity to total capital falls below 2 percent, the OCC must place a bank in receivership or conservatorship within 90 days of notifying the bank that it is critically undercapitalized, unless such action would not achieve the purpose of PCA. This notification occurs during a capital call meeting. When a bank has been critically undercapitalized for 270 days, a receiver or conservator must be appointed, unless the OCC and the FDIC certify that the bank is viable and not expected to fail. An expanded discussion of the issues associated with critically undercapitalized banks is provided in the "Resolution Management" section of this document.

A bank that is critically undercapitalized may not take the following action without FDIC approval:

- Undertake material transactions, except in the usual course of business.
- Extend credit for any highly leveraged transaction.
- Make any material changes in accounting methods.
- Undertake covered transactions as defined in 12 USC 371c.
- Pay excessive compensation or bonuses.
- Pay interest on liabilities above prevailing market rates.

Other Requirements

Most of the actions discussed previously may be taken on the basis of the bank's PCA category and, therefore, require no additional just cause. However, for certain discretionary actions, the OCC must make specific determinations that those actions are necessary to avoid excessive risk to the bank. For example, before the OCC can order a bank to terminate an activity, it must determine that the activity's continuation poses excessive risk to the bank. The OCC must make those determinations in writing. All such determinations must be reviewed by WSRC.

When the bank is less than well-capitalized, its financial condition must be monitored at least quarterly to determine whether the bank is in compliance with its CRP and any other restrictions; and whether its actions are improving identified problems. Those quarterly reviews must be documented in work papers and the OCC's electronic database.

PCA Directives

PCA directives may be issued to impose discretionary PCA restrictions on undercapitalized, significantly undercapitalized, and critically undercapitalized banks. As a matter of policy, PCA directives should be used when the bank is not subject to an existing enforcement action that addresses the current problem or when modifications to an existing enforcement action are needed. The directive will include a capital article that requires specific capital ratios. Prior notice is given to the bank on PCA directives, and the bank can appeal the notice.

III. Resolving Liquidity Problems

To remain viable, a bank must have liquidity — the ability to obtain cash for operations when needed at a reasonable cost. Managing a bank's liquidity during a crisis, particularly when difficulties arise and its financial deterioration is known to the public, can mean the difference between an orderly return to stability and an acute crisis, including insolvency. Examiners should be prepared to deal with wide-ranging liquidity events caused by actual or perceived problems in any area of the bank. As with pending capital insolvency, preventing liquidity insolvency may include a combination of both discretionary and mandatory supervisory actions.

Examiners must monitor and influence bank management's reaction to a liquidity crisis. Many options are available, and certain steps must be taken. Bank management must manage assets, liabilities, and off-balance-sheet cash flows. Further, managing the release of information to the public is as important as managing the bank's financial positions and cash flows. The public's perception of a bank's condition, and thereby the safety of customer deposits, can change quickly, because of negative news (whether substantiated or rumored) about the soundness of a bank's condition. Customer reaction, which is difficult to predict, will influence needs for on-hand liquidity and access to contingency sources. Bank management should have effective processes in place to monitor and react to the contraction of deposits and other funding.

A. Causes of Impairment

As previously noted, liquidity is the ability to obtain cash for operations when needed at a reasonable cost. Cost in this context can be associated with either an acceptable cost of funds or the ability to fund without the sale of desired assets or the disruption of significant lines of business. The critical component in evaluating a given firm's susceptibility to liquidity risk is market confidence in the entity's overall financial condition and reputation.

Recent secular shifts in bank funding activities have made the management of liquidity risk more challenging for banks and more dependent on marketplace perceptions. Historically, banks relied upon traditional core demand, savings, and time deposits as primary funding sources. These deposits generally represented a stable and low-cost source of funds. In recent years, however, statutory changes and the general availability of alternative investment and savings vehicles has made these core deposits more volatile, expensive, and generally less available.

Bankers must adjust to this secular shift in funding by becoming more disciplined and effective liquidity risk managers. In addition to an evaluation of the sensitivity of deposits and other liabilities, bank management must also assess the liquidity of its assets and the effectiveness of associated policies and procedures. If managed effectively, this secular shift may result in increased diversity among funds providers, and greater access to professional market funds at a variety of tenors. Thus, increased market funding alternatives may provide banks with greater flexibility in managing their cash flows and liquidity needs.

The increased reliance on market funding sources at the expense of core deposits poses significant risks and challenges to banks. Institutional fund providers and other market-based sources are significantly more price and credit sensitive than retail customers. Institutional customers are simply less willing to provide funds to banks facing real or perceived financial difficulties. Additionally, reliance on market funding sources makes banks more susceptible to general or regional economic conditions. For example, the Asian crisis of 1997 and the collapse of the Russian ruble in 1998 resulted in increased volatility and reduced liquidity in various capital market products. If not managed properly, market-based funding may be merely a more volatile and expensive source of liquidity, if available at all. Increased interest expense associated with wholesale funding may have a profound effect on bank net interest margins.

A strong positive correlation exists between real or perceived asset quality problems and liquidity problems. Market confidence in a given bank's financial condition is a critical element in assessing liquidity risk, especially for those institutions reliant on wholesale market funding sources. It should come as no surprise, therefore, that liquidity crises at individual institutions generally occur after marketplace awareness of existing or expected erosion in asset quality, earnings, and capital.

Statutory Considerations

Examiners must consider the effect of relevant statutes in assessing liquidity risk. In certain cases, these provisions will eliminate eligible funding sources for banks. These statutory restrictions are triggered by declines in regulatory capital. This serves to strengthen the correlation between asset quality problems and liquidity problems.

As discussed previously, FDICIA established a capital-based supervisory scheme that requires regulators to place increasingly stringent restrictions on banks as regulatory capital levels decline. Various provisions of that statute, and its implementing regulations, directly affect bank liquidity. The most significant liquidity-related provisions are summarized as follows. For additional information on these provisions, examiners are encouraged to contact subject matter experts in Bank Supervision Policy, Special Supervision and Fraud, and the Law Department.

Brokered Deposits (12 CFR 337.6)

- Adequately capitalized banks must apply for and receive a waiver from the FDIC before they can "accept, renew or roll over any brokered deposit." Moreover, the effective yield on these brokered deposits cannot be more than 75 basis points greater than the yield on a comparable deposit offered in the normal market area. Further, for deposits accepted outside the normal market area, the effective yield cannot exceed 120 percent of the current yield on similar maturity U.S. Treasury obligations plus 75 basis points, or, in the case of any deposit at least half of which is uninsured, 130 percent of such applicable yield. Banks should monitor rates weekly.

- Significantly undercapitalized and critically undercapitalized banks may not accept, renew, or roll over any brokered deposit. Further, such institutions may not solicit deposits with an "effective yield more than 75 basis points above the prevailing market rate."

Federal Reserve Discount Window (12 CFR 201.4)

- Undercapitalized banks may not have discount window advances outstanding for more than 60 days in any 120-day period.

- Critically undercapitalized banks may have discount window advances only during the five-day period that begins on the day they become critically undercapitalized.

Interbank Liabilities (12 CFR 206)

- Institutions must implement and maintain written policies and procedures designed to prevent excessive exposure to any individual correspondent institution, based on the capital strength of the correspondent. All institutions must monitor the financial health of their correspondent institutions, taking into consideration capital, nonaccrual and past due loans, earnings, and other factors. The lending institution may rely on another party, such as a rating agency, for this information. Based on the analysis, institutions must establish limits on their financial exposure to correspondents.

- Under 12 CFR 206, the maximum exposure limit is 25 percent of the borrowing bank's total capital, unless the lending institution can demonstrate that its correspondent is at least as adequately capitalized as it is. If levels of capitalization match (and are at least adequately capitalized), the limitation increases to 50 percent.

B. Liquidity Risk Management

Banks and examiners typically can use two distinct discretionary tools in the management of liquidity — a funds flow analysis and a contingency funding plan (CFP). Although those tools should be included in any effective liquidity risk management system during normal times, they are critically important during a crisis. The funds flow analysis depicts a bank's historical sources and uses of funding and provides a general sense of funding activity and trends. The contingency funding plan is a forward-looking document that projects sources and uses of funding under alternative scenarios, when adverse circumstances exist for both the bank as well as the capital markets. (Refer to the Funds Flow Analysis (Appendix F) and Contingency Funding Plan Summary (Appendix G)).

The funds flow analysis and contingency funding plan should be tailored to the specific institution. Furthermore, if the bank already produces the information contained in those reports, but in another format, that information should be used rather than imposing a separate format. In any case, examiners must obtain the information necessary to monitor and manage liquidity.

Funds Flow Analysis

Examiners can monitor liquidity by completing a funds flow analysis. The analysis should be tailored to ensure that significant balance sheet items are incorporated clearly. Because most banks centrally manage their liquidity risk and positions, these analyses typically reflect the condition of the consolidated organization. The reporting format used should allow examiners to distinguish bank from nonbank assets and liabilities. Banks or their parent companies should be able to provide a funds flow analysis and other critical data daily upon request with no more than a one day lag time.

Specific items that should be reported in the funds flow analysis can vary, depending upon the size of the bank and the structure of its activities. For example, a smaller bank that does not have foreign deposits should tailor the report to reflect its particular liabilities. Moreover, absolute accuracy is not required, as a trade-off to obtaining the information promptly. Error tolerance levels can be established, monitored, and controlled. Often, data obtained through peripheral systems, rather than general ledger systems, is acceptable. The funds flow definitions, included in Appendix F, are intended as a guide, but the bank should provide additional details to ensure accurate interpretation by all users.

Contingency Funding Plan

A CFP helps ensure that a bank or consolidated company can manage fluctuations in liquidity prudently and efficiently. (Refer to Contingency Funding Plan Summary (Appendix G).) The plan is an extension of ongoing liquidity management objectives that follow:

- Maintenance of an appropriate amount of liquid assets.
- Measurements and projection of funding requirements during various scenarios.
- Management of access to contingency funding sources.

The degree and sophistication of a CFP should be commensurate with the bank's complexity, risk exposure, activities, products, and organizational structure. All CFPs should also include at least one scenario in which the bank is no longer designated investment grade — when the solution is not merely to raise deposits or borrow additional funds. Further, for larger banks at least one scenario should also consider how the bank would obtain funds in the event of a generally adverse capital market.

Examiners should analyze the CFP to ensure that the bank can control daily liquidity risk. The CFP should show that the bank can obtain sources of funds to cover its uses. Such sources should be identified and listed in the order that they will be approached. The plan should include, as a last resort, borrowing from the Federal Reserve discount window.

Examiners should monitor management's implementation of the CFP. Management should reassess regularly the underlying assumptions in the CFP. If the actual funding events are not realized as planned in the bank's projections, management should revise its contingency plans. However, if management is unable to make the necessary revisions, examiners must influence management to adjust its actions.

If the CFP projects that there may be more uses of funds than sources in a near-term scenario, management should reduce the imbalance immediately. The bank has some basic options to reduce the imbalance:

- Reduce assets that require funding (*e.g.*, the loan portfolio).
- Replace credit-sensitive liabilities (*e.g.*, public funds or other deposits that exceed $100,000) with more stable, credit insensitive funding, such as term retail deposits.
- Lengthen the duration of liabilities.

There are many ways to manage liabilities and assets. Retail deposits can be attracted by increasing the yields offered or by accessing the broker market consistent with the requirements of the brokered deposits regulation, 12 CFR 337.6, discussed earlier. In addition, borrowings from correspondent banks can be increased (*e.g.*, fed funds purchased) consistent with the requirement of 12 CFR 206, discussed earlier. The issuance of new debt is also an option, but it is usually extremely difficult for the bank to disclose adequately its true financial condition in a visibly deteriorating situation. In contrast, assets can be managed by using marketable securities to enter into a repurchase agreement. Various assets may also be used to collateralize FHLB advances. Banks may also suspend new loan originations or manage loan renewals. Another option is to participate out both outstanding loans and those in production. For example, mortgage loan originations can be sold into various government and private securitization programs. As a last resort, assets (loans) can be pledged against borrowings from the Federal Reserve discount window.

Given the importance of liquidity to the viability of the bank, the board must be kept informed about the bank's liquidity position and associated risks. Management should inform the board periodically of the bank's liquidity exposure and its contingency funding plans. Depending on the circumstances, the board may need to receive frequent updates about the plan's development and implementation.

Monitoring Requirements

OCC monitoring can be an effective process in assessing potential liquidity insolvency. The level and frequency of monitoring depends on the severity of a bank's liquidity position.

Examiners should make and update assessments of an institution's level of liquidity risk and quality of risk management as conditions change. Changes in the assessments should be communicated to senior OCC management as they occur. If bank management is not responding adequately to the bank's liquidity situation, appropriate supervisory action should be taken. It may be necessary to impose a formal enforcement action.

For banks experiencing serious liquidity problems, examiners should provide regular reports on the bank's current position to appropriate District/Washington management. Those reports should include information on the adequacy of short-term asset positions and contingency sources relative to short-term liabilities and erosion trends. If applicable, information should be provided on the parent (nonbank) and bank levels. Distinctions are necessary because of legal restrictions and because the parent is typically more sensitive, and often more vulnerable, to market resistance than is the bank.

Examiners also should provide information on the company's longer term liquidity position and prospects. This will include cash flow projections depicting the estimated volume and timing of funds flows and the effect of offsetting liquidity enhancement programs, such as asset sales. Those reports are designed to provide early warning of discount window usage or insolvency in the absence of outside support. Examiners should perform periodic assessments of the volume and types of uninsured funding.

C. Liquidity Crisis Management

If the liquidity risk encountered by the company becomes more pronounced, examiners should consider correspondingly more dramatic supervisory responses. Specifically, examiners should consider the responses discussed in the following paragraphs and be prepared to communicate with: bank management; OCC management; other regulators; and, other banks.

Detailed examples of information to be used in the monitoring and evaluation of liquidity during a crisis may be found in Appendix H.

Supervisory Responses and Communications with Bank Management

In banks experiencing significant liquidity problems, examiners should, in conjunction with bank management:

- Assess the severity of an identified liquidity problem and determine an appropriate regulatory response.

- Determine the liquidity problem's cause, likely public perception, and the bank's ability to respond.

- Orchestrate management's coordination of liquidity on a centralized basis throughout the company, if necessary, to ensure that all assets and liabilities are used at maximum efficiency. Access to the discount window normally will be discouraged until all available internal sources are consumed.

- Assess significant asset divestitures and other strategic changes. If restriction of asset divestitures is warranted, examiners should consider the use of formal enforcement tools to achieve this purpose. (See "Corrective Action Overview" section.)

- Evaluate the feasibility and desirability of the bank setting up a quiet safety net from cooperative commercial or investment banks. This will provide a troubled bank with funds to broadcast into money markets and possibly keep major funds providers from cashing in as they view support. Distinctions should be made between those institutions willing to provide support on a short-term unsecured basis and those requiring collateral.

- Analyze the bank's trading and off-balance-sheet commitments and identify counterparties. Discuss a plan to close out or wind down open positions, if necessary, and determine how to handle matched books. Prompt action will minimize contagion to other financial markets.

- Assess the cash available at all drawing locations. Bank management will need to implement systems capable of identifying needs accurately in terms of volume, currency types, and timing. Logistical issues, such as transportation vehicles, must also be considered. Efficiency here is essential to neutralize public concerns and prevent panic among insured depositors.

- Evaluate feasibility of the bank reducing the exposure of funds providers through "netting" arrangements. This should also be considered for other types of exposures to minimize contagion to other markets and financial institutions.

Supervisory Responses and Communications with OCC Management

To facilitate the OCC's internal communications and decision making, examiners should:

- Alert OCC Press Relations of potential or real liquidity problems. This will prepare them for public and media inquiries and enable them to respond promptly and accurately when appropriate. A unified representation must be made to the media and the public, if warranted, with the concurrence of the FDIC and other regulatory agencies.

- Establish an expedited process allowing high level OCC managers to review and approve transaction requests quickly. This would include divestiture proposals, strategic initiatives, and transactions with affiliates. Consideration should be given to whether the company could be viable after divestiture requests are granted. A streamlined process will permit more effective crisis management.

Supervisory Responses and Communications with Other Regulators

Liquidity problems may require close coordination with other regulators. Examiners should:

- Inform other regulatory agencies of a potential liquidity crisis, as appropriate. OCC management should also communicate with applicable foreign central banks where affected U.S. institutions are based. Subsequent regulatory efforts should be coordinated closely and synchronized logically.

- Work with the FDIC in evaluating the bank, including the value and marketability of its assets. This may involve discussion with FDIC agents and potential acquirers.

- Discuss bank contingency funding plans with the Federal Reserve, including the nature of bank assets pledged for any discount window borrowing.

Supervisory Responses and Communications with Other Banks

In some instances, liquidity problems at one or more banks may prompt additional monitoring of, and communications with, other banks. Examiners should consult with their supervisory office and appropriate lead and Washington experts to determine whether broader monitoring efforts are required. Such efforts may include:

- Implementing liquidity monitoring programs in affected banks, as well as those that are likely to incur subsequent liquidity pressure. Whenever possible, program implementation should take place in anticipation of a critical period or before an actual crisis.

- Ensuring that monitoring of Euromarket reactions is ongoing and communicated to Washington and to affected bank EICs by examiners headquartered in London.

- Establishing high level regulatory communications with CEOs of other major banks to allow them to prepare for possible negative repercussions. This would be particularly critical in a large bank or systemic crisis scenario.

- Prepare for receivership or conservatorship, coordinating with SPSF and LAW.

Resolution Management

If a bank's continued viability becomes doubtful or the bank's condition or behavior otherwise warrants consideration of receivership, the federal banking agencies will begin the process of resolution management. This does not mean that the bank is certain to fail — any reasonable opportunity for the bank to correct its problems and avoid closure is duly considered — but regulators must consider and prepare to implement bank failure contingency scenarios.

This section will provide an overview of the supervision of banks with an increased likelihood of failure because of capital depletion. It will also briefly discuss the other grounds for which a bank can be placed in receivership, as well as other early resolution methods. These materials highlight supervisory issues related to the line review process, the need for a careful record to support receivership, the capital call meeting for critically undercapitalized banks, the bid process, legal review prior to closing, and the formal bank closing procedures.

I. Supervisory Responsibilities for Problem Banks

A. OCC Supervisory Office

The Special Supervision/Fraud unit (SPSF) has been given the responsibility to supervise the resolution of critical problem banks through rehabilitation or orderly resolution management. [16] Ideally, SPSF should assume supervisory responsibility of a deteriorating problem bank prior to its becoming a composite "5" CAMELS rated entity. The supervisory office should consult with SPSF about possible early transfer of responsibility for companies experiencing significant problems. SPSF automatically assumes supervisory responsibility once a bank is downgraded to a "5." This change in supervisory offices must be documented in the OCC's electronic database.

Once it assumes responsibility, SPSF directs the overall supervision of the problem bank, with assigned field examiners working under the direction of an SPSF analyst. The supervision of a problem bank is a time-intensive process. ADCs, EICs and other assigned field examiners should recognize these time requirements when planning supervisory activities, with other non-critical responsibilities diverted to others. Ongoing supervision can include daily liquidity monitoring and the regular review of a bank's financials for movements in the balance sheet or further depletion of capital levels. Field examiners assigned to problem banks could also be responsible for the development of ongoing strategy, off-site reviews, and input into the development of various enforcement actions.

B. Coordination with Other Regulators

As a matter of policy, the federal banking agencies place a high priority on working together to identify and reduce regulatory burden and duplication and, where appropriate, to coordinate supervision and examinations activities. The passage of the Gramm-Leach-Bliley Act (GLBA)

---

[16] This function resides with the Large Bank Division for designated "large banks."

will necessitate communication and coordination efforts among both primary and functional regulators to ensure an orderly resolution of the bank. Through these efforts, the agencies recognize each other's legitimate oversight responsibilities. The need for this type of interagency coordination is even greater for problem and failing banks. Examiners assigned to problem banks must communicate with the other regulators early in the resolution process. Responsibility for interagency communication is shared among the supervisory office, the assigned ADC, and the EIC.

Consistent with their respective statutory mandates, the FDIC and the FRB both have important roles in problem bank supervision. The FDIC, as insurer and receiver, has numerous responsibilities for failing and failed institutions. Also, 12 USC 1818(t) grants the FDIC back-up enforcement authority for certain insured institutions that are in an unsafe or unsound condition or otherwise pose a risk to the deposit insurance fund. Further, under 12 USC 1820(b)(3), the FDIC has special examination authority for certain insured depository institutions. Use of these powers has been rare because of less formal cooperative arrangements between the agencies; however, the FDIC may cite such authorities to seek direct participation in OCC examination activities of problem banks. The Comptroller has reserved to himself the sole authority to deny such a request from the FDIC. If FDIC staff still wishes to examine the bank, they must make a case before the FDIC Board.

The FDIC also is responsible for managing receivership operations and for ensuring that failing institutions are resolved at the least cost to the deposit insurance fund. Whenever a federally insured depository institution fails, the FDIC is immediately appointed receiver and sets about settling the affairs of the bank. This includes balancing the accounts of the institution immediately after closing, transferring assets and liabilities consistent with agreed upon resolution plans, and determining the exact amount of payment due the acquirer and depositors, if any. As will be detailed later, this responsibility necessitates significant pre-closing coordination between the OCC and FDIC.

The FRB's supervisory interest in problem banks is premised on their roles as "lender of last resort" and holding company supervisor. FDICIA significantly curtailed the FRB's ability to lend to problem banks. As stated earlier, under 12 CFR 201.4, Federal Reserve Banks may only make discount window advances to undercapitalized banks for no more than 60 days in any 120-day period. Critically undercapitalized banks may receive discount window advances only during the five-day period that begins on the day it becomes critically undercapitalized.

II.   Asset Quality and Line Review Process

Increases in problem loans and assets, and resulting increases in required ALLL balances, are the most frequent cause of banks' becoming undercapitalized and later falling into the critically undercapitalized capital category. Loan and other asset write-ups that provide support for required chargeoffs and ALLL provisions are essential in establishing the bank's accurate capital levels and thus determining whether grounds for closing the bank are present. A line review process validates these examination findings by ensuring that asset classifications, and the approach and methodology used to arrive at the required ALLL balance are consistent with OCC policies and procedures. This process is summarized as follows.

A. Asset Write-Ups

The decision to write-up an asset depends on:

- Bank management's concurrence with the classification.
- Whether an insider loan is involved (write-up usually recommended).
- The size of the asset being classified relative to the total assets of the bank.
- The dollar amount of the classification.
- Complexity of the asset.

Usually some form of write-up for assets that reflect Loss or Doubtful classifications will be required. Write-ups for significant substandard loans or loans with large specific ALLL provisions are also necessary. All write-ups must be concise, clear and support fully the rating decision because of the possibility of a legal challenge.

Detailed write-ups may not be necessary for every asset included in the Summary of Criticized Assets ROE schedule. Small loans and other assets identified as doubtful or loss often are not written-up. Rather, bullet points that concisely state the reasons for classification are generally acceptable. These summary documents often use descriptive phrases such as "Unable to Meet Repayment Program," "Insufficient Collateral Values," or "Questionable Repayment Source." Smaller loans and other assets with similar characteristics may be grouped under one heading for classification. For example, the heading may be "Severe Past Due Status and Unsecured," with the name of each loan or other asset itemized under that heading. Information provided on the other assets within the bank that are classified include itemized lists of other real estate owned, accrued interest, repossessions, investments, and cash items. At times, detailed write-ups on these assets may be necessary.

B. Line Reviews

Since accurate classification of assets is critical to the bank's survival, a line review process exists to verify identified losses independently. As previously noted, the line review validates examination findings by ensuring that asset classifications are consistent with OCC policies and procedures. The line review also serves as a quality assurance process in that other examiners not involved in the examination validate and review the examination findings. This process ensures that the decisions made during the on-site examination are not arbitrary, inconsistent with OCC examination policies and procedures, or based on the opinion or decision of one person.

The line deck consists of the work papers and write-ups used to document information concerning the assets reviewed during the examination, especially those classified substandard, doubtful, or loss. Information submitted for the line review consists of the "Summary of Criticized Assets" page, loan or other asset write-ups and supporting documentation, and the ALLL analysis and supporting documentation.

This information for the line review should be submitted by the EIC to the SPSF analyst. Participants in the line review will be experienced examiners, who have not been involved directly in the current bank examination. Usually, the SPSF analyst responsible for the bank participates as one of the reviewers. Depending on the nature of the exam findings, types of assets classified, and management/board reaction to the exam findings, the EIC or OCC management may decide to include additional recognized "experts" on the review team. Attendance of those additional examiners for the line review will be left to the discretion of the EIC and ADC.

Each write-up is reviewed and discussed. A determination is made about whether to agree or disagree with the criticism. When necessary, the review team will adjust criticized amounts or require enhancements to write-ups to provide better support to the criticism. The review team will also consider management's opinion of the criticism, any allocated ALLL provision, collateral values, and dates of the last appraisal, inspection, or other valuation in making its determination.

Since capital-based closings are tied to the level of equity capital, the review to validate the results of the ALLL analysis is critical. The ALLL methodology, with supporting documentation, should be submitted for review, along with the recommended ALLL balance and provision.

If the participants in the line review are unable to reach agreement on the classification of specific assets or the ALLL provision, other senior examiners or the Director for SPSF will decide the issue. Generally, few significant changes to classifications or required provisions occur during line review because of the extensive reviews conducted by personnel during the examination or within the field office. If changes do occur, the EIC makes them in preparation for the capital call meeting.

III. Grounds for Receiverships and Early Resolution

The OCC has authority and responsibility to appoint a receiver for a national bank (which will be the FDIC if the bank is insured) for a number of grounds, discussed below. There is similar authority to appoint a conservator for a bank. PCA also gives the authority for the OCC to require the sale or merger of a bank in certain circumstances. The agency's goal is to resolve an institution in a manner that avoids or minimizes losses to the deposit insurance funds.

The most commonly used grounds for receivership have been:

- The bank's assets are less than its obligation to its creditors (capital insolvency).
- The bank is likely to be unable to pay its obligations or meet its depositors' demands in the normal course of business (liquidity insolvency).
- The bank is critically undercapitalized.

For a receivership based on capital insolvency or critically undercapitalized status, accurate assessment of capital is crucial, as discussed above. Management of those failures follows the procedures discussed in this section. Monitoring for the potential for a liquidity insolvency and the management of liquidity failures require customized procedures similar to those contained in the "Liquidity Crisis Management" section appearing earlier in this booklet.

The OCC also has the authority to place a bank into receivership before the bank becomes critically undercapitalized if one or more of the specified grounds exists. Such action may help resolve a problem bank at the least long-term cost to the federal deposit insurance funds. Early resolution can reduce or limit losses that might otherwise result if the bank is allowed to remain open until its capital has dropped below 2 percent. Early resolution can be considered, for example, when a bank is: losing capital, has no realistic prospects for recapitalization, or is engaging in practices likely to increase losses in the future. Moreover, even in situations where the bank is adequately- or well-capitalized under PCA, receivership may be appropriate if there are substantial unsafe and unsound practices the bank is not addressing or there are other significant failings identified in the receivership statutes.

The other receivership grounds can be divided into three groups. The grounds for receivership are set out in 12 USC 191 and 1821(c)(5). First, there are other <u>grounds related to capital</u> (in addition to capital insolvency and critically undercapitalized bank status):

- The bank has incurred, or is likely to incur, losses that will deplete all or substantially all of its capital, and there is no reasonable prospect for the bank to become adequately capitalized without federal assistance.
- The bank is undercapitalized and (1) has no reasonable prospect of becoming adequately capitalized, (2) fails to become adequately capitalized when required to do so, (3) fails to submit a capital restoration plan acceptable to the OCC within the time period prescribed, or (4) materially fails to implement its capital restoration plan.
- The bank otherwise has substantially insufficient capital.

Second, there are <u>grounds based on violations of law or unsafe or unsound practices</u> that have had, or are likely to have, a substantial negative effect on the bank:

- There is substantial dissipation of assets or earnings due to any violation of statute or regulation or any unsafe or unsound practice.
- There is a violation of law or regulation, or an unsafe or unsound practice or condition, that is likely to cause insolvency or substantial dissipation of assets or earnings, weaken the institution's condition, or otherwise seriously prejudice the interests of the bank's depositors or the deposit insurance fund.
- The bank is in an unsafe or unsound condition to transact business.

Third, there are <u>grounds based on a variety of critical management failures</u> of the bank:

- The bank's board of directors has fewer than five members.
- There is a willful violation of a cease-and-desist order which has become final.
- There is concealment of the bank's books, papers, records, or assets, or refusal to submit the bank's books, papers, records, or affairs for inspection to any examiner or to any lawful agent of the OCC.

- The bank, by resolution of its board of directors or its shareholders, consents to the appointment.
- The bank ceases to be an insured institution.
- The Attorney General notifies the OCC in writing that the bank has been found guilty of a criminal money laundering offense.

The OCC can appoint a conservator for a bank generally for the same grounds as a receiver. However, conservatorship is rarely used. In addition, in some circumstances the OCC may require a bank to be sold to another holding company or to merge with another bank. Under PCA, if a bank is significantly undercapitalized or is undercapitalized and has failed to submit and implement a capital restoration plan, then the OCC may require the sale or merger of the bank, if one or more grounds exist for appointing a receiver. Apart from PCA, in appropriate instances, the OCC also can discuss the advisability of sale, merger, or voluntary liquidation with problem banks.

When a bank becomes undercapitalized or when a bank begins to show the substantial safety and soundness or other failings indicated in the receivership grounds, but is not yet critically undercapitalized, supervisory offices should consider whether an early resolution contingency plan involving sale/merger or receivership, would be appropriate. This could be the case, for example, when a bank has reached the point beyond which additional enforcement or PCA is not likely to prevent continued deterioration and failure or reduce costs associated with it. Once a decision is made to adopt an early resolution approach, OCC resources should be focused on the best available option at the least cost to the deposit insurance funds. The facts and reasons on which the receivership grounds are based must be well supported and documented. In most instances, prior enforcement or PCA will have addressed these matters at an earlier stage, before they became more severe (*e.g.,* when the bank first became undercapitalized or when the bank was required to remedy unsafe and unsound practices in an enforcement action). The record prepared for those actions will later be a part of documenting the receivership grounds. Additional documentation of the continuation and worsening of problems, and for some grounds documentation of the substantial negative impact on the bank's assets, earnings, and/or ability to conduct business will be needed. All OCC offices involved in early resolution planning (*e.g.,* appropriate bank supervision, corporate licensing, and legal offices) should be apprised of the possible need to take steps to support early resolution. Examiners should consult with these units regarding options available and what record will be needed to support them.

IV. Bank Closing Process

A. Capital Call Meeting for Critically Undercapitalized Banks

A capital call meeting is scheduled when a determination is made that a bank is critically undercapitalized. This normally occurs after the line deck review confirms the appropriateness of the critically undercapitalized status. In many respects, the capital call meeting signals the beginning of the closing process for a critically undercapitalized bank. Given the ramifications to the bank, the Director of SPSF will usually conduct the meeting, assisted by the SPSF analyst and EIC. The EIC must understand the purpose of the capital call meeting, the effects on the bank, and assist in the preparation of the Capital Analysis Worksheet (see Appendix I). The EIC also should be prepared to present briefly the results of the examination. Because of the bank's capital position and imminent failure, a report of examination is not written in advance of the capital call meeting. However, results of the examination are presented briefly at the meeting.

During the capital call meeting, the board will be informed that, as a result of losses identified during the examination, the bank is critically undercapitalized. The board is given a letter notifying the bank officially of their capital category and warned that only limited time is available to increase inadequate capital levels. The letter reports the bank's tangible equity ratio and declares that under section 12 USC 1831o, the OCC is required, within 90 days of this notification, to appoint a receiver or a conservator for the bank, or take whatever action it determines, with the concurrence of the FDIC, that would better achieve the purposes of prompt corrective action. Although typically banks are placed into receivership within 90 days, rare extensions are given when a capital injection is imminent. Banks also may be closed sooner than 90 days if the bank's condition warrants it.

The board will then receive a capital analysis sheet that provides notice of the minimum capital injection needed to restore adequate capital to the bank. A copy of a capital analysis sheet is provided within Appendix I. This sheet is prepared prior to the capital call meeting by the EIC and SPSF analyst after losses have been confirmed by the line review. After discussing capital needs, efforts are made to determine the status of plans to obtain additional capital. The OCC reiterates to the board that it welcomes any viable and realistic plan that will restore adequate capital to the bank.

Additional items in the failure process also are discussed with the board. Depending on the type of bid transactions offered, an FDIC representative attends the meeting to obtain the board's execution of the Access Resolution. The Access Resolution authorizes the FDIC to bring potential bidders into the bank to perform a due diligence review. For the failure to be the least disruptive as possible, the FDIC needs early access to bank information to assemble an informational package for potential bidders.

Lastly, participants must discuss the sensitivity of the information. They must warn the board that rumors and speculation in the local community can cause a liquidity crisis, and that, therefore, the board must plan and monitor liquidity.

B. Bid Process

The FDIC begins to market the failing bank, after gathering necessary information and determining the appropriate resolution structure. The FDIC invites all approved bidders to an information meeting to encourage competition. Normally, this meeting will occur a week or two after the capital call meeting. After signing confidentiality agreements, bidders receive copies of the informational bid package, including financial data on the institution, legal documents, and other documents describing the various resolution methods being offered. The FDIC discusses at the meeting, the details of the failing institution, the materials included in the informational bid package, the due diligence process, and the bidding procedures. The OCC, as chartering official, will describe certain regulatory requirements for bidding and the application process for branches or new charters of national banks. The transaction terms typically are focused on the treatment of the deposits and assets held by the failing bank. Potential bidders usually are given a day or two to express their interest in bidding on the bank.

If necessary based on the type of transaction, the FDIC schedules on-site due diligence by prospective bidders. The number of bid groups allowed to perform a due diligence review of the bank at any one time is based upon space availability in the bank. The presence of an OCC examiner during the on-site due diligence normally is not required, since an FDIC representative will be on hand in the bank. The prospective bidder is not allowed to ask bank management for assistance or clarification in the review of the loan and other asset files. Confidentiality is extremely important, and all bidders are advised of the penalties for any breaches.

The length of the due diligence period depends on the interest expressed. Once the finish date for the last bidder due diligence review is known, a tentative closure date is identified and discussed with the FDIC. The resolutions bid process involves determining which bid is least costly to the insurance fund and working with the acquiring institution(s) through the closing process, or ensuring the payment of insured deposits in the event there is no acquirer. The closure date can be changed due to the circumstances or the submission of a realistic and viable recapitalization plan. This tentative date is not disclosed to the bank.

C. Other Examiner Responsibilities

During the 90 days prior to closing, examiners may be assigned a variety of tasks. Among them are:

- Reviewing the FDIC bid process.
- Monitoring the bank's condition.
- Entering information on the closing bank into the OCC electronic database.
- Assisting SPSF analysts to complete the "Resolution Worksheet and EIC Information Questionnaire," described in the next paragraph and contained in Appendix J.
- Assisting in the preparation of the charge-off letter for the closing book and providing information for OCC senior management confirming the propriety of any receiver's declaration.
- Providing input to the Bank Failure Questionnaire (see Appendix K), which records information about each bank failure. This information will be compiled and analyzed later in the OCC's periodic failed bank studies.
- Responding to possible questions from various OCC divisions, senior management, FDIC, and the press about the closing. Inquiries from the press should be directed to the OCC's Press Relations Division.
- Assisting in the development of a ROE in the event the bank survives.

D. Legal Review

The "Resolution Worksheet and EIC Information Questionnaire" is used by the Law Department to prepare required opinions, declarations, and decision documents in advance of closure. Even before examiners fill out the "Resolution Worksheet and EIC Information Questionnaire," during the early resolution contingency planning, examiners need to coordinate with SPSF and LAW in developing documentation for the reasons for the receivership. The "Resolution Worksheet and EIC Information Questionnaire" is forwarded by the assigned SPSF analyst to the Bank Activities and Structure (BAS) Division, which coordinates the legal review of a problem bank's failure. BAS advises the analyst on the legal issues raised by the closing and prepares the closing documents for the bank. In addition, BAS notifies the Litigation Division (LIT) of the closing and forwards to the assigned LIT attorney a copy of the Worksheet/ Questionnaire. The SPSF analyst and BAS attorney must stay in regular contact, especially in the two weeks leading up to a scheduled closing.

Reasons or grounds for closure and documentation for the grounds are included in the required materials surrounding a bank closing. Ideally, the SPSF analyst and BAS and LIT attorneys should meet to discuss the legal grounds that support the receivership and to clarify the facts on which particular grounds depend. The OCC's Law Department verifies that the grounds listed are accurate, that the facts support the listed grounds, and that there is sufficient documentation of facts for court review. Most banks have several grounds listed in their documentation.

LIT prepares a Declaration that is sworn under oath by the Director of SPSF and that sets forth the factual and legal underpinning for the receivership appointment. The assigned BAS and LIT attorneys work together to ensure that the closing documents and Declaration are consistent and that each is legally and factually supportable. The closing documents and Declaration are prepared in draft for review by the SPSF analyst and SPSF Director. Once they are finalized, the Director signs the Declaration and the assigned SPSF analyst briefs the Senior Deputy Comptroller (SDC) for Bank Supervision Operations on its contents and requests that the SDC execute the closing documents. The reviewing attorneys may be asked to attend that briefing. The closing documents are executed in dated and undated form. The undated documents can be used, if the closing is delayed.

LIT also compiles an official record of the decision to close the bank. The record is the administrative record of the OCC's action and is used to defend the agency's action if it is challenged in court. When appropriate, LIT works with BAS, the Director of SPSF, and the EIC to prepare the defense. In such cases, the LIT coordinates its actions with the appropriate United States Attorney's Office.

The assigned SPSF analyst and BAS attorney are responsible for ensuring that all documents required for the closing are prepared and distributed. The analyst also maintains ongoing communication between the bank, the FDIC, and various divisions within the OCC that are involved in the closing. The analyst prepares all other required notification letters and the draft press release. He or she also creates the Closing Book containing all of the documents and other information related to the closing (see Closing Book Table of Contents in Appendix L). Finally, the analyst generally serves as the on-site Closing Manager on the day the bank is closed.

Even after all of the previously mentioned preparations for closing have occurred, the OCC can still stop the closure process at any time up to the actual moment the bank is placed into receivership. A bank in the Southeast received a cash wire at the last moment that brought capital above minimum levels and allowed it a few months to raise additional capital. The closing was stopped, even though the FDIC was already poised to receive the bank and had housed approximately 60 examiners in hotels in the area.

E. Bank Closing Day Procedures

Banks are typically closed at the end of the normal business day on Friday, with an OCC representative in each branch office. If under new ownership, the bank normally reopens the following Monday to ensure continuity of operations and access to customer deposits.

Because of its significance, the actual closing process is a tightly structured process. At the end of the normal business day for the bank and each branch office, the OCC's decision maker, typically a senior deputy comptroller (SDC) acting as a designee of the Comptroller, holds a teleconference with the on-site EIC. An attorney from the OCC's Law Department may also participate in the teleconference. A formalized set of questions is used to verify the propriety of the decision to place the bank into receivership (see Appendix M). The SDC asks if the lobby is cleared and if the bank has completed its business day. Questions are asked about the bank's capital, total assets, capital ratios, and capital category. A question is also asked about the existence of any reasonable prospect for the bank to become adequately capitalized without federal assistance. An affirmative answer to this question could halt the closing at the last moment. However, if all of the answers show the bank to be critically undercapitalized with no reasonable prospects for recovery, the SDC appoints the FDIC receiver for the bank. The OCC delivers appropriate closing papers to the bank and the FDIC to complete the transfer. As part of the closing process, the OCC recovers the original bank charter (see Appendix N for Closing Procedures).

V.   FDIC's Basic Resolution Methods

There are three basic resolution methods for failing institutions. These are deposit payoffs, purchase and assumption transactions, and open bank assistance transactions.

A. Deposit Payoff

A deposit payoff occurs when the OCC has appointed the FDIC as receiver and there is no purchaser for the bank's insured deposits, or the FDIC determines that a deposit payoff is the least costly resolution method. The FDIC, as insurer, pays all of the failed institution's depositors the full amount of their insured deposits up to the $100,000 insurance limit. Depositors with uninsured funds and other general creditors of the failed institutions do not receive either immediate or full reimbursement; instead, the FDIC, as receiver, issues receivership certificates to uninsured depositors. A receivership certificate entitles its holder to a portion of the receiver's collections on the failed institution's assets. The percentage of claims eventually received depends on the value of the bank's assets, the number of uninsured claims, and each claimant's relative position in the distribution of claims.

B. Purchase and Assumption Transaction

A purchase and assumption (P&A) transaction is a closed bank transaction in which a healthy institution (generally referred to as either the acquirer or the "assuming" bank) purchases some or all of the assets of a failed bank and assumes some or all of the liabilities, including all insured deposits. As a part of the P&A transaction, the acquirer usually pays a premium to the FDIC for the assumed deposits, which decreases the FDIC's total resolution cost.

The passage of FDICIA compelled the FDIC to consider more transaction options to make certain that all plausible least cost options were considered. As a result, the FDIC has considered a number of P&A structures in the resolution of failed banks. These structures ranged from a "clean P&A" that passed few assets to the acquirer, a "whole bank P&A" that passed virtually all assets, to a "modified P&A" that required the acquirer to purchase the cash and securities, and portions of the installment mortgage loan portfolios. Most significantly, FDICIA eliminated the presumption that all deposits were to be passed to acquirers. All-deposit transfer bids are now at a relative disadvantage to insured deposit-only transfer bids. After FDICIA, the FDIC would only use an all-deposit P&A if the purchase premium paid by the acquirer offset the additional cost to the FDIC of protecting uninsured liabilities. Additionally, the FDIC attempts to reduce resolution costs by selling assets pools to banks that are not assuming deposits, selling a failed bank's branches to different banks, and entering loss sharing agreements on certain asset pools.

In exigent situations, the FDIC may be appointed receiver prior to a final determination of the structure of the P&A or the identification of the winning bidder. In these instances, the FDIC can use its "bridge bank" authority to continue banking operations until it is ready to resolve the failed bank. A bridge bank is a special kind of national bank chartered by the OCC and controlled by the FDIC. The assets and liabilities of the failed bank (which is in receivership) are transferred into the bridge bank. The bridge bank operates like a normal bank as far as customers are concerned. Then, when the FDIC is ready, it moves on to final resolution, either by selling the bridge bank to the winning bidder or by failing the bridge bank and having a P&A transaction with the winning bidder.

C. Open Bank Assistance Transaction

In an open bank assistance (OBA) transaction, the FDIC, as insurer, provides financial assistance to an operating insured bank or thrift determined to be in danger of failing. The FDIC can make loans to, purchase the assets of, or place deposits in a troubled institution. When possible, an assisted institution is expected to repay its assistance loan.

OBA is no longer a commonly used resolution method. Only seven such transactions have occurred since 1989 and none, since 1992. These transactions ceased because of problems experienced in certain transactions, especially because of lengthy negotiation process required, and legislative changes. These legislative changes restricted the use of OBAs, primarily through the least cost requirements, and broadened the alternatives available to resolve large bank failures, such as bridge bank authority.

Accounting Issues in Problem Banks

Numerous accounting issues are identified routinely in the resolution of problem banks. Generally, those banks will be striving to increase earnings and reduce operating costs to regain profitability and increase capital. To achieve those results, some banks may attempt to reduce losses or increase income inappropriately. If improper accounting principles are applied, significant misstatement of financial results and regulatory capital may occur. Therefore, examiners should watch for aggressive accounting positions taken by management. A delay in the identification of improper accounting practices could result in misleading financial information. Examiners should focus on the key accounting issues of asset valuations without reasonable basis; failure to follow accounting rules requiring write-downs; and, inaccurate financial reports. Those and other issues are discussed more fully in the following paragraphs.

I.   Asset Valuations without Reasonable Basis

A variety of asset valuation issues may be encountered during the supervision of a problem bank. A bank may adopt overly aggressive accounting estimates, value assets improperly, or enter into unusual or related party transactions in an attempt to reduce losses or realize large gains to offset losses from other transactions. Potential areas of abuse are described in the sections that follow.

A. Loan Sales

Consistent with FASB Statement No. 125, "Accounting for Transfers and Servicing of Financial Assets and Extinguishment of Liabilities," banks may record servicing rights and other retained interests and recognize a gain in a loan sale or securitization. Such retained assets are recorded based on their relative fair value. Because such assets are extremely sensitive to the underlying assumptions used to determine fair value, income could be overstated if the fair values assigned to such assets are inflated. For example, a bank unjustifiably may use low loss severity factors and low market discount rates, expected low default rates, or low prepayment rates when valuing those assets. In these circumstances, the values assigned may need to be adjusted downward. Accordingly, the method and key assumptions used in valuing servicing assets and other residual interests should be evaluated to determine whether they are appropriate.

Unforeseen market events can affect discount rates or the performance of receivables supporting such retained assets. Accordingly, these assets must be reviewed periodically for impairment (significant decrease in value). This resulting revaluation can affect earnings and capital. The best evidence of fair value is a quoted market price in an active market. If quoted market prices are not available, the fair value may be estimated. If the fair value of such retained assets is significantly less than the recorded book value, the assets must be reduced to their current fair value by a charge to earnings. Accordingly, examiners should be alert for assumptions that, although originally reasonable, cannot be justified by current market rates or conditions. Discount rates and key assumptions underlying fair values should be identified and evaluated to determine if they are still appropriate. If bank management cannot provide objectively verifiable support for the valuation of the retained interest, the portion of the asset not supported by fair market value will be classified as loss and disallowed as an asset of the bank in financial and regulatory reports. For additional discussion of this issue, please see the Problem Bank Identification section of this document and OCC Bulletin 99-46, Interagency Guidance on Asset Securitization Activities (December 16, 1999).

B. Related Party Transfers

Banks also transfer impaired assets to related parties to recognize gains or avoid losses. For example, banks have transferred bank premises or other assets to insiders in exchange for promissory notes. In some cases, those transfers do not reflect the true economic results, and the likelihood of full repayment is uncertain. Also, assets have been exchanged for limited partnership interests solely to purchase the bank's properties. Such transfers should be viewed carefully to ensure that the sales price is not above market values, especially if the buyers are known by or are heavily indebted to the bank.

When assessing the property-related asset exchange transactions just mentioned, the partnership interest acquired should be valued based on the fair value of either the OREO or partnership interest, whichever is more clearly evident (typically, the current market value of the real estate is the best indicator). However, the bank should record a loss on the transfer if the carrying amount of the OREO exceeds the established exchange value. The transfer would indicate a gain if the exchange value was greater than the net carrying amount of the OREO. The gain must be deferred, because the exchange is not a culmination of the earnings process (for accounting purposes). In addition, any cash received would be applied to reduce the carrying amount of the limited partnership interest. After the exchange, the bank should account for its investment in accordance with AICPA Statement of Position No. 78-9, "Accounting for Investment in Real Estate Ventures." Generally, this requires that the bank use the equity method of accounting for its limited partnership interest.

C. Sale and Leasebacks

Problem banks also enter into sale and leaseback transactions to recognize gains and increase capital. In such a lease transaction, a portion of the gain applicable to the bank's leaseback must be deferred. However, the lease term often does not represent the intent of the parties involved in the transaction. Accordingly, examiners should be alert for sale and leaseback transactions with an arbitrarily short leaseback term. Terms on these transactions increase significantly the amount of income that can be recognized, but do not reflect the intended use of the property. Typically, the lease term is expected to be close to the remaining useful life of the asset leased.

D. Loss Carry Forwards and Deferred Tax Assets

Problem banks often seek to maximize their income and capital by recording deferred tax assets for the estimated future tax effects that arise from deductible temporary differences (future reductions in taxable income) and net operating loss carry forwards. Current accounting standards allow the recognition of those future tax benefits, but they should be reduced, if necessary, to the amount that is more likely than not to be realized. Realizability of those assets generally is more questionable for a bank that has incurred recently a large loss or has had a period of losses over the last few years. In those situations, the bank's potential ability to obtain a tax refund is an important consideration. Further, such benefits that depend on future taxable income are limited for regulatory capital purposes to the lesser of the amount that is expected to be realized within one year or 10 percent of Tier 1 capital.

In addition, examiners should look for transactions in which the bank's parent company forgives its deferred tax liabilities. The motivation for this transaction is to report a negative tax, thereby increasing income. Those transactions lack economic substance, because the parent legally cannot relieve the subsidiary of a potential future obligation to the taxing authorities.

E. Bonding Claims

Problem banks experiencing fraud and fidelity losses can have future recoveries from insurance coverage. However, because bonding policies are complicated and contain numerous exceptions, it is generally a long time before such claims are resolved and anticipated insurance proceeds, if any, are received. Accordingly, such claims are generally considered gain contingencies and are not recognized before a written settlement offer has been received from the insurer. Examiners should review insurance claims carefully to determine that actual losses are recognized currently and not deferred, because of the possibility of future recovery. However, a bonding claim may be recorded in advance when collection is probable and the amount can be estimated reasonably. The particular facts and circumstances of each case must be evaluated when determining these conditions.

F. Other Transactions

Service contracts — Other transactions intended to reduce losses or increase capital improperly can include long-term service contracts to pay costs in excess of market. These contracts are often made on the condition that the vendor purchase assets at inflated prices or make an immediate capital investment in the bank. The vendor is compensated for those transactions through higher than market future service fee contracts. These agreements should be accounted for in accordance with their economic substance without regard to its legal terms.

Capital stock sales — Banks should not inappropriately increase their capital by selling stock in exchange for loans. Such notes received in exchange for capital stock should not be recorded as assets. Rather, generally accepted accounting principles (GAAP) require that they be recorded as a deduction from stockholders' equity, unless they are secured by irrevocable letters of credit or other liquid assets (e.g., certificates of deposit) and are paid within a reasonably short period of time (i.e., 90 days or less). Hence, the increase in capital is reduced by the amount of the notes received as payment for the stock.

Loan origination costs — Banks also should not increase income and capital improperly by capitalizing higher than appropriate loan origination costs. Financial Accounting Standards Board Statement No. 91, "Accounting for Nonrefundable Fees and Costs Associated with Originating or Acquiring Loans and Initial Direct Costs of Leases" (FAS 91), allows only certain direct loan origination costs for completed loans to be deferred. The deferred amounts are offset against loan fees and the net amount is amortized to income over the life of the related loan.

Overhead costs, such as advertising, soliciting, and administrative costs should not be deferred. Rather, they should be charged to expense in the year incurred. Examiners should watch for significant costs that do not qualify for deferral.

Nonaccrual — Banks must immediately place loans on nonaccrual status when full repayment of interest and principal is not expected, or when loans become 90 days or more delinquent and are not both well secured and in the process of collection. This may affect income and capital since interest income generally is not recognized during the period a loan is on nonaccrual status. In addition, previously accrued and unpaid interest generally should be reversed out of interest income.

Essentially, the accrual of interest income is suspended when a loan becomes 90 days or more past due, unless it is both well secured and in the process of collection. In determining when a loan is in the process of collection, a 30-day collection period generally is applied. A longer period may be acceptable, however, if the timing and amount of repayment is reasonably certain. Because of the uncertain collectibility of loans on nonaccrual, interest payments received are applied against the loan's carrying amount. However, interest income may be recognized on a cash basis, when recovery of the recorded loan balance is reasonably assured.

Examiners should determine whether banks analyze their loan portfolio to determine which loans must be placed on nonaccrual, and that necessary reversals of interest earned not collected are recorded promptly. This should be done at least quarterly. Examiners should also check to see whether the recorded loan balance is fully collectible for those loans for which interest income is recognized on a cash basis.

Related party loans — In addition, examiners should question the guarantee by the bank's parent for claims or advances to related parties that have remained outstanding for unusually long periods of time. This should be done to determine the reasonable expectation of collection and whether a charge off is appropriate.

II.   Transactions Inconsistent with Accounting Rules for Write-Downs

A. Other Real Estate Owned

Financial difficulties of borrowers may result in foreclosure or repossession, with the bank becoming an owner and subsequent seller of other real estate. Those properties must be recorded upon foreclosure at their fair value, less selling cost, with the difference between the recorded amount of the loan and the fair value of the property (less cost to sell) charged to the allowance for loan losses. Any future write-downs of OREO should be charged against operations. GAAP requires that OREO pending sale be carried at the lower of this new cost basis or fair value less selling costs on a property-by-property basis. Examiners should be alert for efforts by problem banks to avoid losses by using inappropriate or stale appraisals to value such properties. Also, 12 CFR 34 establishes the time limit for holding such properties. Any extensions require regulatory approval.

Some banks have sold real estate to reduce OREO through transactions that do not meet the requirements of FASB Statement No. 66, "Accounting for Sales of Real Estate" (FAS 66). In many of those situations, the banks indirectly provided the borrower with the funds to make the down payment. However, the cash down payment requirement of FAS 66 can be satisfied only with the borrower's personal funds, funds borrowed from an unrelated source, or an irrevocable letter of credit from a third party. This requirement for a cash down payment generally is not met when a bank provides the borrower with an additional loan for working capital or when the borrower's down payment is obtained by draws on an unrelated line of credit with the bank.

Some banks have also attempted to recognize income on real estate sales transactions that have inadequate down payments. To qualify as a sale under the full accrual method of accounting, the minimum down payment and other requirements under FAS 66 must be met. Other accounting methods may be used in accounting for sales of real estate; however, income recognition is generally deferred.

Banks have also facilitated the sale of foreclosed properties by providing a loan at less than current market interest rates. In that situation, Accounting Principles Board Opinion No. 21, "Interest on Receivables and Payables," requires that the loan be discounted to bring its yield to a market rate. The effect of the discount will be to either increase the loss or reduce the gain on sale.

B. Troubled Loan Restructurings

To reduce nonperfoming assets and maximize their recovery, banks will often work with borrowers experiencing financial difficulties to restructure their loans. Those workout strategies generally involve a modification of terms and are made to improve a loan's collectibility. However, the collectibility of future payments in a restructuring may be questionable. Therefore, a credit evaluation should be performed to determine if any additional amounts should be charged to the allowance for loan losses.

Additionally, if a concessionary interest rate or principal reduction is granted because of the borrower's financial difficulties, the restructuring may require that impairment be recognized under FASB Statement No.15 (FAS 15), "Accounting by Debtors and Creditors for Troubled Debt Restructuring" (as modified by FAS 114, "Accounting by Creditors for Impairment of a Loan"). FAS 15, as amended, requires that impairment be measured based on the present value of the expected future cash flows, discounted at the effective interest rate in the original loan agreement. Alternatively, impairment may be measured based on the loan's market price or the fair value of the collateral. Impairment generally is measured by using a valuation allowance.

Also, the restructuring of a loan by itself generally does not warrant returning a loan immediately to accrual status. When a loan is restructured, the borrower must demonstrate the ability to comply with the new terms. Accordingly, a period of payment performance (generally six months) is required before returning the loan to accrual status. However, if the borrower had been making payments (for six months) equal to those required by the restructured loan agreement, immediate return to an accrual status may be appropriate.

C. Reclassifying Loans as "Held for Sale"

Other transactions intended to reduce the level of reported nonperforming assets or reported loan losses can include reclassifying loans as "held for sale." Use of this account may be appropriate in certain circumstances. However, some banks transfer loans to this account in an attempt to reduce or mask the reported level of problem or nonaccrual assets. The transfer may also be used in an attempt to reduce reported charges to the ALLL. If the loan(s) is on a nonaccrual status prior to, or subsequent to it being transfer to the "held for sale" account, the loan(s) should continue be included with other nonaccrual loans for regulatory reporting.

At the time a decision is made to sell loan(s), the loan(s) should be clearly identified and transferred to a "held for sale" (HFS) account. The transfer to the HFS account must be made at the lower of cost or fair value in the period in which the decision to sell is made. Any reduction to reflect the loan's lower market value that is *primarily* attributed to credit factors should be recorded as a charge to the ALLL. However, if the decline results *primarily* from interest rate fluctuations or changes in foreign exchange rates, it should be recorded as a charge to a non-interest expense account. When a decline in value results from both credit and market factors, the primary factor should be determined. In such situations, the entire write down should be accounted for based on this determination. In almost all cases, the decline in value of commercial loans is generally due to credit factors. Accordingly, in most instances the decline in value is charged to the ALLL.

D. Impaired Loans and the Timing of Asset Loss Recognition

As other companies, problem banks must recognize losses on impaired loans on a timely basis. Detailed guidance for evaluating impaired loans is contained in FAS 114, "Accounting by Creditors for Impairment of a Loan" and in various supervisory guidance, including the Interagency Policy Statement on the Allowance for Loan and Lease Losses (ALLL Policy Statement) and the Allowance for Loan and Lease Losses booklet of the *Comptroller's Handbook*. Examiners should reference the Interagency Policy Statement on the Review and Classification of Commercial Real Estate Loans, (November 7, 1991) and the "Commercial Real Estate and Construction Lending" booklet of the *Comptroller's Handbook*, when reviewing troubled, collateral dependent loans. Generally, large commercial loans are evaluated individually for impairment. If a loan is not collateral dependent, impairment is generally based on the present value of expected future cash flows discounted at the loan's effective interest rate.

Problem banks may also attempt to delay improperly the actual charge-off of credit losses. GAAP requires that identified losses be charged off against the ALLL in the period that they become uncollectible. Delaying recognition of losses into another reporting period misstates the bank's ALLL, regulatory capital, and historical loss experience. The bank's overall ALLL is generally included in Tier 2 capital, subject to a limit of 1.25 percent of risk-weighted assets. Accordingly, examiners should be alert for large loan and other asset write-downs occurring shortly after the end of the year or the end of a quarter. If evidence of loss was or should have been available prior to the end of a reporting period, the bank must report the write-down in that previous period.

III. Disclosures in Financial Reports

A. Reporting Errors

Bank management and directors are responsible for the Call Report and other financial information reported to shareholders, depositors, and the general public. The reports should be complete, accurate, and conform to generally accepted accounting principles and regulatory requirements.

Information about its financial performance is especially important for a problem bank. Because of the sensitivity to a problem bank's current financial condition, management may be slow to recognize losses, or may omit or obscure poor financial results and disclosures that may indicate increased risk and deteriorating financial condition. For example, some banks will not appropriately disclose significant gains and losses, pending litigation, ALLL levels or chargeoffs, and other financial information. Those disclosures are especially critical to the supervision of a problem bank. If not disclosed and dealt with promptly, the potential exists for problems to worsen and ultimately impair the bank's earnings, liquidity, and capital. Accordingly, examiners should ascertain as soon as possible that Call Report and other external information are accurate and those important disclosures are properly included. This can be achieved through ongoing reviews of quarterly financial results and the verification during examinations of financial reports, such as the Call Report.

B. Window Dressing Activities

Banks also may attempt to engage in transactions that increase their risk-based capital ratios inappropriately. This may include the sale of impaired or high risk-weighted assets, which the bank agrees to buy back shortly after the reporting date. As a result, the bank's risk-based capital ratio is increased on reporting dates. Other key ratios, such as those involving the ALLL, may also be affected. Examiners should be alert for the possible indication of undisclosed repurchase agreements and transactions that reverse shortly after Call Report dates.

Problems in Large and Multi-Charter Banking Companies

The resolution of supervisory problems within large and multibank banking companies presents unique challenges. In addition to the risk issues discussed earlier in this document, supervisors typically must assess the ability of the holding company to support bank operations legally; the condition of commonly controlled depository institutions; and the potential systemic risk posed by the bank's failure. Statutory changes, introduced by FDICIA and largely untested since implementation, will result in significant changes in the way the OCC resolves large problem companies. Although regulatory discretion is reduced under this new regime, examiner judgment is still critical to the successful resolution of a large problem company.

In assessing supervisory options for the resolution of large problem companies, it is useful to consider the changes to the supervisory landscape since the last economic downturn in the 1980s and early 1990s. Two fundamental changes have occurred in this time period. First, substantial changes were enacted in relevant laws, regulations, and supervisory policies. Many of them were discussed earlier in this document. Second, industry consolidation has created a number of extremely large, diversified financial institutions. Their size and breadth will affect the systemic risk analysis associated with large problem companies. We will discuss both of these supervisory landscape changes to provide a context for the present supervisory regime for large problem companies.

I.   Resolution of Large Problem Banks — the "Old Way"

Large banks are subject to U.S. banking laws and regulations in the same manner as community banks. However, regulators have always considered additional factors before closing or otherwise resolving large failed banks, because of the size and scope of their operations. The ultimate fate of a large problem bank involved a delicate balance between reliance on market discipline and an assessment of the systemic risk resulting from failure. Prior to legislative changes in the late 1980s and early 1990s, the systemic risk assessment often proved more compelling, resulting in numerous government-assisted transactions involving large banks that protected the interests of depositors.

The fundamental difference between the failure of large and community banks is the resulting impact of the failure. The closure of a large bank could affect the entire industry and overall economy adversely by causing widespread depositor withdrawals at other banks; failures of downstream correspondent banks and other creditors; and impairment of public confidence in the broader financial system. This, in turn, could lead to serious disruptions in domestic and international payment and settlement systems. These and other concerns compelled regulators to look for alternatives to merely closing a bank and paying off insured depositors. The consideration of those alternatives by regulators resulted in the development of what came to be known as the "Too-Big-To-Fail" (TBF) doctrine.

The TBF doctrine significantly influenced the resolution of large banks in the 1980s and early 1990s. Literally speaking, those banks actually may not have been too big to fail, but they were too big to close and liquidate in the conventional way. Instead, regulators opted for managed shrinkage, merger, or recapitalization as the preferred means of dealing with large problem companies. In many cases, this resulted in government protection of all uninsured depositors.[17] This implicit government support of depositors further eroded market discipline for problem companies.

Regulatory policy at the time reflected this preference for a managed shrinkage, merger, or recapitalization. Under its then-existing cost test, the FDIC was required only to select the resolution method that was less costly than the payoff of insured deposits and liquidation of assets. Moreover, the FDIC was permitted to provide open-bank assistance, regardless of cost considerations, if the bank's services were determined to be "essential" to the community. Those options allowed the FDIC to extend selectively federal protection of deposits beyond the official limit of $100,000 per account, per institution.

Another important tenet of supervisory policy during the 1980s and early 1990s downturn was the Federal Reserve Bank's (FRB) so-called "source of strength" doctrine. Under this policy, each bank holding company had an affirmative requirement to "serve as a source of financial and managerial support to its subsidiary banks." This doctrine was set forth in both policy guidance and regulation, and the FRB used it to require some bank holding companies to downstream capital to faltering subsidiary banks in the early 1990s. [18] In light of other supervisory tools authorized by FDICIA, it is doubtful that the FRB would use that doctrine in the same way today.

Another significant influence on the problem bank resolution process for large banks during the 1980s was Federal Reserve discount window advances. Federal Reserve banks had broad authority under Regulation A, 12 CFR 201, to advance funds to depository institutions that did not have other sources of credit and liquidity. Before FDICIA, the FRB's discretion to allow the Federal Reserve banks to serve as the "lender of last resort" was not restricted by statute. Supervisors used this authority to provide temporary liquidity to banks experiencing problems, as well as a vehicle to manage the failure process to facilitate an orderly liquidation. The collateral requirements imposed by Regulation A served to insulate the FRB from the risk of loss.

---

[17] From 1979 to 1989, the FDIC protected 99.7 percent of all depositors at failed commercial banks.

[18] See FRB Statement of Policy dated April 24, 1987, and 12 CFR 225.4(a) (1997).

II. Resolution of Large Problem Banks — Today

From 1987 to 1991, Congress enacted three major pieces of banking legislation[19] that significantly changed the supervision of problem banks. Among other things, these statutes altered the level of discretion accorded regulators in the supervision of depository institutions and bolstered their enforcement powers. The resolution of large banks still involves balancing an assessment of systemic risk with the application of market discipline; however, these statutory changes, especially those found in FDICIA, altered this balancing toward a greater emphasis on market discipline. Within this context, however, the proper exercise of supervisory discretion remains a critically important aspect of the resolution of large problem companies.

As noted earlier, large banks are generally subject to U.S. banking laws and regulations in the same manner as community banks. In the problem bank context, this means that large banks are subject to the capital and liquidity restrictions outlined in the "Rehabilitation of Problem Banks" section of this guide. Also as with community banks, early identification and communication of problems is critical to the successful resolution of a large problem company. However, examiners must focus on certain unique issues with large banks, even in the earliest stages of the resolution process.

A. Asset Quality Problems

Banks experiencing significant asset quality problems resulting in capital impairment will fall within the constraints imposed by the PCA provisions of FDICIA. As was discussed in the "Rehabilitation" section, although bank regulators can and should use non-PCA-based supervisory restrictions to address supervisory concerns, the mandatory restrictions imposed by PCA define the discretionary parameters for supervisory actions.

The statutory and regulatory framework of PCA established a capital-based supervisory scheme that requires regulators to place increasingly stringent restrictions on banks as capital levels decline. (See the "Resolving Credit and Capital Impairment Problems" section for a discussion of those mandatory restrictions.) Because the PCA mandatory restrictions are triggered by capital ratios that historically have been lagging indicators of bank condition, examiners routinely analyze considerably more information than regulatory capital ratios in assessing a bank's condition. Therefore, based on examiner assessment of condition and problems, the OCC would normally impose formal actions on banks before they become subject to the mandatory provisions of PCA.

Capital Restoration Plan

One of the most significant requirements in the PCA framework is the need for undercapitalized banks to file an acceptable CRP. (See the "Resolving Credit and Capital Impairment Problems" section for a discussion of the minimum elements of an acceptable CRP.) As described in OCC

---

[19]   The three major laws were the Competitive Equality Banking Act (CEBA); Financial Institutions Reform, Recovery and Enforcement Act of 1989 (FIRREA); and Federal Deposit Insurance Corporation Improvement Act of 1991 (FDICIA).

Bulletin 94-43, dated June 29, 1994, the OCC may not accept a CRP submitted by an undercapitalized bank, unless each company that controls the bank has: (1) guaranteed that the bank will comply with the plan, until it has been adequately capitalized on average during each of four consecutive calendar quarters; and (2) provided appropriate assurances of performance. The aggregate liability under those guarantees, however, is limited under PCA. Section 1831o and 12 CFR. 6.5(i) limit the aggregate liability of all controlling companies for capital restoration plan guarantees to the <u>lesser of</u>:

- Five percent of the bank's total assets at the time the bank was notified, or was deemed to have notice, that it was undercapitalized, or

- The amount necessary to restore the bank's capital to the levels required for the institution to be adequately capitalized, as those levels were defined at the time the bank initially failed to comply with its capital restoration plan.

The guarantee should, at a minimum, provide the holding company's financial commitment and appropriate assurances of performance to the OCC that the company's subsidiary bank will comply with the bank's CRP. (See Appendix D for additional discussion on the requirements of a holding company guarantee of a CRP, and Appendix E for a sample CRP guarantee.)

As discussed earlier in this section, regulators previously used the source of strength doctrine to compel holding companies to support troubled subsidiary banks; however, this doctrine has been called into question by the courts. This was evident in a lawsuit brought by the bankruptcy trustee ("Branch") for Bank of New England Corporation creditors. In that case, the court determined that holding company attempts to provide tangible capital support to significantly troubled subsidiary banks constituted a fraudulent conveyance under the Bankruptcy Code.[20] The court determined that holding company creditors, especially bondholders, suffered damages as a result of these transfers of assets to the bank.

More recently, a provision of GLBA attempted to address the banking agencies' exposure to liability highlighted in the Branch decision, and its impact on the use of the source of strength doctrine for problem companies. Specifically, section 730 of GLBA amended the Federal Deposit Insurance Act by adding 12 USC 1828(t). This new section enhances the source of strength doctrine by, in certain circumstances, protecting the federal banking agencies and the deposit insurance funds from claims brought by the bankruptcy trustee of a depository institution holding company or other person for the return of capital infusions into problem banks.

The practical effect of "Branch" and the new legislation is still unresolved. Because of that uncertainty, examiners should consider the possibility that the holding company guarantee of the capital restoration plan may be the only support from the holding company on which the bank can reasonably rely.

Assessing a holding company's commitments under a CRP requires consideration of the method by which the holding company has provided, and intends to fulfill, its "appropriate assurances of

---

[20]   See Branch v. FDIC, C.A. No. 19-10976 (E.D. Mass. 1998).

performance." In the case of a cooperative, strong holding company controlling an undercapitalized bank, the OCC might accept a bank's CRP with only a written guarantee from the holding company along with a copy of its audited financial statements. In other cases, a pledge of nonbanking assets may be required. For example, a financially weak holding company that controls an undercapitalized bank generally will be required to pledge assets to secure its guarantee. Similarly, a holding company that controls a significantly or critically undercapitalized bank generally will be expected to include a contractual pledge of assets, regardless of financial strength.

Cross-guarantees

Another important supervisory tool that is particularly relevant to the resolution of large and multicharter problem companies is the cross-guarantee authority enacted in FIRREA. Under this authority, an insured depository institution can be held liable for any loss that the FDIC expects to incur in connection with the default of a commonly controlled, insured depository institution.[21] Those provisions, granted to address problems encountered in the resolution of certain large banks in the 1980s, effectively prevents banks from shifting assets and liabilities in anticipation of failure of one or more affiliated insured banks.

Unlike the PCA provisions, the banking agencies have experience in using the cross-guarantee authority in the resolution of large problem companies. This authority was first used with Maine National Bank (MNB), a subsidiary of Bank of New England Corporation. In that situation, the FDIC demanded immediate payment from MNB of an amount equal to the FDIC's expected loss as receiver of Bank of New England, N.A. When MNB was unable to make the payment, the OCC declared it to be insolvent and placed it in receivership.[22]

One of the most instructive examples of the use of cross-guarantee authority was in the 1992 closure of the bank subsidiaries of First City Bancorporation of Texas, Inc. In that situation, two of the First City banks were insolvent, which led to the FDIC assessing claims against the other 18 subsidiary banks. The value received in the cross-guarantee claims was significant. Ultimately, the deposit insurance fund incurred no loss as a result of the closure of the First City subsidiary banks.

The cross-guarantee authority has certain inherent limitations. This provision authorizes the federal banking agencies to assess liability against any "insured depository institution" for losses incurred in connection with the default of a commonly controlled bank. Accordingly, if a bank is placed into receivership resulting in an expected loss to the FDIC in its receivership capacity, the FDIC can cover that loss by making claims against affiliated banks — there is no ability to seek redress from the holding company for those losses. This insulation of holding companies and their nonbank affiliates from the cross-guarantee claims is an important fact to be considered in

---

[21] The cross-guarantee provisions are found at section 5(e) of the Federal Deposit Insurance Act, 12 USC 1815(e).

[22] The FDIC has settled a case brought by the trustee in bankruptcy for Bank of New England Corporation creditors concerning an issue unrelated to the banking agencies cross-guarantee authority. The use of cross-guarantees is still a legitimate and useful supervisory tool for multibank companies.

the resolution of multibank companies. For example, if a holding company pledge of assets is considered necessary in the approval of a capital restoration plan, consideration should be given to requiring the pledge of nonbank-related assets. In so doing, shareholders of the holding company would stand to lose, not only their entire investment in the failed banks, but also a substantial portion of any remaining value in the holding company.

B.   Liquidity Problems

The fundamentals of identifying, measuring, monitoring, and controlling liquidity risk at large and multibank companies are essentially the same as previously described in the "Resolving Liquidity Problems" section earlier in this booklet. Similarly, the changes imposed by FDICIA on funding options for troubled depository institutions applies equally to all bank companies licensed in the United States. The scope and scale of potential liquidity problems at large and geographically dispersed banking companies, however, present unique challenges to examiners. Moreover, the international nature of certain business and funding activities of these companies necessitates more intricate coordination and an understanding of the requirements of multiple legal and political jurisdictions.

The large scale of some bank operations will increase the difficulty of determining the extent of any liquidity problems; the effects of such problems on the condition of the company; and public perception of the situation. It may also complicate the resolution decision for a specific problem or troubled institution.

Banks operating in other countries generally do so under prevailing local laws and customs. These operating conditions must be considered in the resolution of troubled banks. Ideally, regularized communications with relevant foreign supervisors will be established well in advance of any identified liquidity problems. In many cases, the OCC will have formally established information sharing agreements and other arrangements designed to facilitate cooperative supervision. In these efforts, significant care should be taken to restrict communications of concerns, plans, and other matters only to appropriate senior personnel to ensure proper confidentiality, perspective, and consistency. The risks and sensitivities associated with cross-jurisdictional and international communications require a high degree of knowledge and diplomacy for efficient and effective resolution.

Finally, while it is important to maintain customer access and minimize disruption to the broader financial markets, care must be taken to balance the need for freedom of funds flows with the need to prevent the "cherry picking" of assets from various legal entities. Appropriate supervisory personnel must establish monitoring mechanisms to ensure the propriety of activities, and when relevant, develop legal or other formal agreements to codify a common understanding among various parties.

To facilitate timely and consistent monitoring of liquidity issues, both domestic and foreign, the OCC's Treasury and Market Risk Division prepares a "Large Bank Liquidity Watch Report" quarterly. This report is a summary of relevant risk ratings and other liquidity-based evaluations of large banking companies. Examiners are encouraged to use this report to see how rating agencies view their supervised institutions and peers and to help identify emerging issues.

Examiners can access this report through the Treasury and Market Risk Division's home page on the intranet.

If the liquidity risk encountered by the company becomes more pronounced, examiners should consider correspondingly more dramatic supervisory responses. In the most severe situations, examiners should perform a systemic risk analysis. Systemic risk considerations are discussed in the next section.

III. Systemic Risk

As was discussed earlier, the closure of a large bank could affect significantly the banking industry and have destabilizing repercussions on the overall economy. Those systemic risk concerns have always figured prominently in the resolution of large problem banks. FDICIA fundamentally altered this systemic risk determination in three ways.

First, FDICIA required bank regulators to choose the "least-cost" alternative in resolving failing banks.[23] An exception to this provision applies to those banks whose failure would cause "serious adverse effects on economic conditions and financial stability." Second, FDICIA significantly limited Federal Reserve discount window advances to troubled banks.[24] This restriction clearly affects the ability of regulators to manage the failure resolution process. Third, as discussed earlier, FDICIA introduced PCA for insured depository institutions. The OCC is required under PCA to appoint a receiver or conservator when such an institution has been critically undercapitalized for 90 days. The OCC may grant up to two 90-day extensions, provided that the OCC and the FDIC concur and document why such extension would better serve the purposes of PCA. If the institution has been critically undercapitalized for 270 days, a receiver or conservator must be appointed unless the OCC and the FDIC certify that the institution is viable and not expected to fail.

FDICIA's "least-cost" test placed significant limits on the level of discretion in the failure management process. Except when a "systemic risk" determination has been made as described later, the FDIC is now prohibited from protecting any uninsured deposits or nondeposit bank debts, when such actions would increase the cost to the insurance fund. In effect, this provision also prohibits the FDIC from providing open-bank assistance to an institution, unless the open-bank alternative was less costly than a closed-bank resolution.

FDICIA provided an exception to the least-cost requirement for systemic risk, but strictly limited the application of the exception. As set forth in statute, an exception to the least-cost requirement is available, only if:

- At least two-thirds of both the FDIC board of directors and the Board of Governors of the Federal Reserve makes a written recommendation in favor of such an exception.

---

[23] Section 141 of FDICIA, 12 USC 1823(c)

[24] Section 142 of FDICIA, 12 USC 347b

- Acting on this recommendation, the Secretary of the Treasury, in consultation with the President of the United States, determines that:

  - Application of the least cost requirement would have sent serious adverse effects on economic conditions or financial stability.

  - The proposed supervisory action would avoid or mitigate such adverse effects.

Although the OCC is not involved in this process directly, it is likely that the agency will participate in the systemic risk assessment — examiners are uniquely qualified to describe the severity of a bank's problems and to estimate the potential "knock on" effects of its failure. Today's large banking companies are not only substantially larger, but more diversified and complex than their predecessors during earlier problem periods. Moreover, expanding powers increase the role of banking organizations in the financial system, making it more likely that the failure of a large institution would be deemed destabilizing. Therefore, in the systemic risk analysis of these companies, examiners would likely be called upon to assist in determining:

- Relevant market shares of the institution by geography and product.
- The number and nature of relationships with correspondent and serviced institutions.
- Potential effects on domestic and international counterparties.
- Potential effects on payment systems.

Problems in Federal Branches and Agencies

Federal branches and agencies are exposed to the same risks that face national banks. However, unlike national banks, branches[25] are merely extensions of the foreign banking organization (FBO). They do not maintain a separate capital base and are not required to maintain a separate allowance for loan and lease losses (ALLL). For supervisory purposes, the capital and the ALLL of the FBO support the federal branch and agency. Therefore, external events that affect the FBO can increase certain risk factors for the branch, such as transfer,[26] liquidity, credit, and reputational risk. Risks associated with FBOs can be entity specific and unique to the FBO or affected by economic and political events in the home country that can lead to systemic banking problems.

Concerns about the financial condition of the FBO can affect the federal branch in several ways:
- An unanticipated withdrawal of third party funding.
- The inability to obtain dollars from the FBO to fund cash outflows.
- Deterioration in asset quality if loans extended by the branch or agency are concentrated in the home country where economic problems are worsening.

The range of supervisory and enforcement tools addressing violations of laws and regulations and breaches of safety and soundness in national banks can usually be used in federal branches. However, when liquidity, transfer, or asset quality risk are of supervisory concern, certain requirements can be included in enforcement actions that are unique to federal branches. These unique tools reflect the wholesale funding and absence of a separate and distinct capital base in branches.

Following is a discussion of the five most frequently used provisions to: (1) ensure that the branch or agency has sufficient liquidity to meet its obligations; or (2) ensure that the branch or agency has sufficient quality assets that can be liquidated over a reasonable period of time to repay third-party liabilities. These provisions often are used to insulate the branch from problems associated with the FBO or in the home country. The decision about which of these provisions should be used depends on the quality of the assets maintained in the United States; the level of home country support provided to the FBO; the nature of the problems in the FBO; and the adequacy of management.

Maintenance of a "Net Due To" Position or a "Neutral Net Due" Position

Federal branches raise funds in the U.S. and can provide these funds to related U.S. or foreign entities, creating a "due from" position (the federal branch is a provider of funds to related entities). Conversely, the related entities may have excess dollar funding, which is placed in the federal branch for investment in the U.S., creating a "due to" position (the federal branch is a borrower of funds from related entities). In most cases, the federal branch is engaging in simultaneous transactions and at any point in time on a net basis may owe money to related

---

[25]   References to branches also pertain to agencies.

[26]   Transfer risk is the possibility that an asset cannot be serviced in the currency of payment, because of a lack of, or restraints on the availability of, needed foreign exchange in the country of the obligor.

entities ("net due to" position) or it may be owed money from related entities ("net due from" position). If the federal branch were to maintain a "net due from" position with financially weak related entities, the federal branch would depend upon recovery of these funds from the related entities to repay U.S. liabilities when the related entities may not be able to access dollar funding. The "net" position is used because in the event of liquidation, money owed by the FBO to the federal branch can be offset against money owed to the FBO by the federal branch. When concerns arise with respect to transfer, liquidity, or credit risks, the federal branch can be required to maintain a "net due to position" for related entities. The required "net due to" position may be expressed as percentage of third-party liabilities. The "net due to" position serves as a cushion against declines in asset values in the event of liquidation. Note that the liquidity position of the branch or agency is enhanced under this provision only to the extent that new funds provided by the FBO to the branch or agency are invested in liquid assets.

Asset Maintenance Agreements

Asset maintenance is defined generally as the maintenance of eligible third-party assets in a federal branch to cover a specified percentage of a branch's third-party liabilities. When used, the asset maintenance ratio has historically ranged between 105 percent to 108 percent, but the level is at the discretion of the OCC. A ratio over 100 percent also means that the federal branch, by default, must maintain a "net due to" position to related parties at all times. An asset maintenance ratio below 100 percent, although rare, would have the effect of limiting the "net due from" related parties position. The definition of eligible assets can vary, but generally consists of quality assets that can be collected over a reasonable period of time in the event of liquidation. As a result, limitations are placed on the amount of classified assets that can be included as eligible assets; for example, the agreement may state that only 80 percent of the balance of substandard assets may be included as eligible assets.

Maintenance of a Positive Asset/Liability Gap Position

The federal branch can be required to maintain third-party assets that mature in conjunction with third-party liabilities or to maintain assets that mature in conjunction with all liabilities, both third party and related. The required maintenance by default, of a positive third-party asset/liability gap position also means that the federal branch must be in a neutral or "net due to" position. When FBO's become financially weak, creditors of the federal branch typically shorten maturities which, without a commensurate change in asset maturities, may result in the branch funding long-term assets with shorter-term volatile liabilities. The maintenance of the positive gap position can be specified by maturity period, for example 180 days, 360 days, or five years. Typically, weekly or bi-weekly reporting to the OCC of the branch's gap position is required.

Higher Capital Equivalency Deposit (CED) Ratio

In accordance with 12 USC 3102(g) and 12 CFR 28.15 and subject to the OCC's discretion, federal branches must maintain a CED of the greater of 5 percent of third-party liabilities or the amount of capital that would be required of a national bank being organized in the same location. The branch can be required to maintain a higher CED ratio, if concerns arise over the solvency of the FBO and the potential exists that the branch may have to be liquidated. The CED serves as a cushion in the event that the liquidation of assets does not fully cover third-party liabilities. Liquid assets held in the CED are pledged to the OCC. Therefore, raising the CED amount does not enhance the liquidity position of the branch.

Liquidity Requirements

The federal branch can be required to maintain liquid assets at a certain percentage of third-party liabilities. A liquidity ratio of 100 percent effectively means that in the event of liquidation or third-party funding withdrawals, the branch has sufficient liquidity to repay these liabilities. In essence, all funds from third parties must be invested in liquid assets, which reduce loanable funds. A ratio of 50 percent would mean that third-party liabilities would have to decline by 50 percent before the federal branch would be forced to liquidate nonliquid assets to meet additional maturing liabilities or obtain funding from the FBO. The federal branch may be allowed by the OCC to count as liquid assets for purposes of calculating the required liquidity ratio those liquid assets held in the CED account. Eligible liquid assets are defined by the OCC when setting the liquidity requirements.

OCC Appeals Process

The board and management may express disagreement with examination findings and various supervisory actions during the supervision of a problem bank. In those cases, examiners should not hesitate to discuss the bank's options under the OCC's appeal process.

OCC Banking Bulletin 96-18, "National Bank Appeals Process," and PPM 1000-9, "Administering Appeals from National Banks," contain the OCC's appeals policy. That material states that a national bank may seek review of appealable matters by filing an appeal with *either* the Ombudsman or the bank's immediate supervisory office. If a bank files the appeal with its immediate supervisory office and is dissatisfied with the appeal decision, it may further appeal the matter to the Ombudsman. In the absence of any extenuating circumstances, the Ombudsman will issue a written response to the appeal within 45 calendar days of receipt. Early contact with the Ombudsman's office by banks and OCC supervisory personnel is actively encouraged and often leads to the resolution of disputes without the need to file a formal appeal.

The Ombudsman has authority, with the prior consent of the Comptroller, to supersede any appealable agency decision or action in the resolution of an appealable matter. Appealable matters include *"any* agency decisions or action, including a material supervisory determination." Examples of material supervisory determinations include those relating to: examination ratings; adequacy of loan loss reserve provisions; and, classifications of loans significant to an institution.

A national bank may *not* appeal to the Ombudsman or its immediate OCC supervisory office: (1) appointments of receivers and conservators; (2) preliminary examination conclusions; (3) enforcement-related actions or decisions, including decisions to take prompt corrective action; (4) formal and informal rulemakings; and, (5) requests for agency records or information under the Freedom of Information Act.

Appeals involving problem banks can arise at almost any stage of the supervisory process. Unless such appeals are barred by one or more of the exceptions previously described, or are resolved satisfactorily through the supervisory office appeal, they will be received and acted upon by the Ombudsman. The Ombudsman's office is aware of the sensitivity and importance of appeals that arise in the problem bank context. Such appeals often involve issues that go to the heart of a bank's CAMELS ratings, which may directly drive various supervisory actions and the ultimate resolution of the bank's problems. A great deal is often at stake in such situations, both for the bank and for the supervisory office. The severity and scope of enforcement and other supervisory actions frequently turn on the component and composite ratings assigned by examiners. Moreover, emotions can run high, and the parties involved can become strongly invested in their positions. Channels of communication with the supervisory office must remain open and operating during appeals involving problem banks.

Because of those considerations, it is the policy of the Ombudsman's office to accord problem bank appeals priority treatment and to take extra care to ensure that the appellate process is not only fair, but as expeditious as possible.

OCC's appellate process is an avenue afforded bankers to challenge pertinent supervisory conclusions. It is not a forum to circumvent necessary supervisory or enforcement actions, nor is it a vehicle to protract the implementation of necessary remedial efforts. During the pendency of a problem bank appeal, the Ombudsman will not hesitate, when appropriate, to exercise the authority to implement any disputed agency decision or action.

Appendixes

Appendix A

Guidance for Supervising Banks Experiencing Rapid Growth

Excessive growth has been recognized historically as an effective early indicator of potential future problems in banks. Problems associated with excessive growth can manifest themselves throughout the bank. They include credit, liquidity, and internal control deficiencies. Significant growth and expansion into new products or activities by banks must be accompanied by a corresponding increase in the level and sophistication of bank risk management systems.

Determination of Excessive Growth

As with most difficult decisions in bank supervision, the determination as to whether growth within an individual institution is excessive is ultimately a matter of examiner judgment. The examiner must assess whether the volume, nature, and type of growth can be managed effectively by the bank in view of its internal control structures, employee skill sets, new product offerings, asset quality, off-balance-sheet activities, liquidity status, and other relevant considerations. Examiners must consider both the quantity of risk and the quality of risk management in all relevant areas.

Numerous tools are available to assist examiners in determining the quantity of risk. Both Project Canary reports and ADC quarterly reports specifically identify banks with excessive growth characteristics relative to peer groups. Among the factors considered in these reports are:

- Annualized asset and loan growth, in both the aggregate and within loan segments.
- Annualized changes in relevant ratios, including ROA, ROE, NIM.
- Annualized changes in OREO and ALLL.
- Annualized changes in risk-based capital and leverage capital ratios.
- Quarterly and annualized changes in off-balance-sheet items.

Growth rates and financial ratios, however, do not indicate the quality of risk management. While examiners should include this empirical data in determining whether growth is an issue within a bank, other more subjective factors must be considered:

- The adequacy of the control environment of the company, particularly within the area experiencing growth.

- The effect of growth on underwriting standards. Asset growth enabled by a reduction of loan underwriting standards, revisions to customer/product risk tolerances, or changes to lending areas or sources of loans, should be a particular concern for examiners.

- The skill sets of employees. The bank must have sufficient depth of management talent to oversee a growth or expansion of business. Particularly for new product offerings or lines of business, the bank must make certain that growth is not beyond the competencies of existing staff and management.

- An assessment of how management will fund growth. Funds management and liquidity issues must be considered by management and examiners. Particular focus should be placed on those banks that use new funding sources, such as asset securitization, to finance growth activities.

- The continued adequacy of the level of, and methodology for, the allowance for loan and lease losses.

- The continued capital adequacy of the bank.

- In addition to the risks directly associated with new or expanded activities, excessive growth also may serve to divert management's time and attention away from controlling existing activities. Examiners must continue to focus on overall risk management and control assessments for banks experiencing significant growth.

Supervisory Response to Rapid Growth

Banks experiencing rapid growth must receive additional supervisory scrutiny commensurate with the nature of the growth and judgment of the supervisory office.

Increased Off-Site Supervisory Focus

At a minimum, all banks experiencing rapid growth should receive additional off-site monitoring. The growth should be assessed relative to the bank's projected growth rates and any previous representations to examiners by bank management. Examiners must opine on the adequacy of risk management controls and management expertise in the off-site analysis. If examiners cannot make this assessment adequately off-site, a targeted on-site examination should be scheduled, preferably within 90 days of the off-site analysis.

Increased On-Site Supervisory Focus

Rapid growth likely also will warrant an increase in the scope and/or frequency of the OCC's on-site examination program. Examiners should expand the scope of the on-site examination to include a more focused review of the area experiencing growth and an expanded assessment of the internal control environment of the institution. Examiners should refer to the relevant booklets of the *Comptroller's Handbook* and other OCC verification procedures for additional guidance and procedures.

Corrective Actions to Address Excessive Growth

Formal or informal enforcement action is normally appropriate if excessive growth has not been accompanied by an appropriate control environment and management oversight. Examiners are encouraged to review the "Corrective Action Overview" section of this document for additional information on the use of OCC enforcement authority.

The presence of excessive growth adds additional weight to the decision to take corrective action against a bank. The following discussions are designed to emphasize the unique issues the supervisory office must consider when taking enforcement actions against banks experiencing excessive growth. These are in addition to the factors discussed in the "Corrective Action Overview" section of this document.

Safety and Soundness Standards

The OCC has the authority under 12 USC 1831p-1 and 12 CFR 30 to issue a safety and soundness order against a bank that fails to meet established safety and soundness standards. Asset growth is among the operational and managerial standards established under Part 30. Pursuant to statute and Part 30, a bank that fails to comply with any of the established standards must file a plan with the OCC to correct the deficiency. If the bank fails to submit an acceptable plan or fails to satisfactorily implement an approved plan, the OCC must, by order, require the bank to correct the deficiency. The use of safety and soundness orders can be an effective tool to supervise more directly banks experiencing excessive growth, especially for banks that are not capital impaired. Examiners should consider use of this enforcement tool for banks experiencing significant growth not accompanied by appropriate management oversight or controls.

Part 30 has unique provisions governing excessive growth that may influence certain enforcement actions undertaken by the OCC. By statute, the OCC may be required to take additional supervisory actions against a bank if its assets increase by more than 7.5 percent during any quarter within the 18-month period preceding the issuance of an OCC request for the submission of a compliance plan under Part 30. Among the possible actions, the OCC may be required to prohibit or restrict the increase in the bank's average total assets during any calendar quarter, or increase the bank's ratio of tangible equity to assets. Examiners are encouraged to contact the Law Department for additional guidance.

Prompt Corrective Action

As set forth in 12 USC 1831o and 12 CFR 6, Prompt Corrective Action (PCA) established a capital-based supervisory scheme that requires regulators to place increasingly stringent restrictions on banks as regulatory capital levels decline. For a certain population of banks, restrictions on the level of growth are mandatory. Specifically, the OCC must restrict the growth of assets for banks within the undercapitalized, significantly undercapitalized, and critically undercapitalized capital categories. Examiners are encouraged to review the "Corrective Action Overview" section of this document for additional information on PCA and to contact the Law Department for additional guidance.

Other Formal and Informal Actions

In addition to the enforcement tools previously discussed, the OCC may use the traditional enforcement powers against national banks to address concerns about excessive growth. Informal actions, such as board resolutions, commitment letters and memoranda of understanding, can be crafted to deal specifically with growth concerns. In more egregious situations, formal actions, such as written agreements and consent orders, can be tailored to specifically address individual bank situations. Examiners are encouraged to review the

"Corrective Action Overview" section of this document for additional information on these enforcement options and to contact the Law Department for additional guidance.

POLICIES & PROCEDURES MANUAL

PPM 5310-3

Comptroller of the Currency
Administrator of National Banks

Section: Bank Supervision   Subject: Policy for Taking Corrective Action

---

To: Deputy Comptrollers, District Administrators, Department and Division Heads, District
Counsel and all Examining Personnel

Purpose

This PPM sets out the OCC's policy for use of its various authorities to carry out its
responsibilities to take appropriate corrective actions in response to violations of law, rules,
regulations, final agency orders and/or unsafe and unsound practices or conditions. It replaces
PPM 5310-3 (Rev.) dated November 14, 1991. This PPM is designed to outline responses
available to the OCC whenever it deems some form of corrective action necessary to address
safety and soundness or compliance issues. This corrective action may take the form of informal
or formal enforcement action under 12 U.S.C. § 1818, prompt corrective action (PCA) under 12
U.S.C. § 1831o, safety and soundness orders under 12 U.S.C. § 1831p-1, or some combination
thereof.

Under the provisions of 12 U.S.C. § 1831p-1, each federal financial institution regulatory agency
is required to promulgate standards for safety and soundness in a number of specified areas.
These regulations are effective as of December 1, 1993. If an institution fails to meet the
standards or fails to submit or implement a plan for compliance with the standards, the agency
must issue an order requiring the institution to correct the deficiencies.

These policies and procedures provide only internal OCC guidance. They are not intended, do
not, and may not be relied upon to create rights, substantive or procedural, enforceable at law or
in any administrative proceeding.

POLICIES & PROCEDURES MANUAL

Comptroller of the Currency
Administrator of National Banks

Section: Bank Supervision   Subject: Policy for Taking Corrective Action

---

General Scope and Policy

A.   Scope

This PPM governs the OCC's use of formal and informal enforcement actions, PCA measures and safety and soundness orders involving national banks and federal branches and agencies ("Banks"). It does not address civil money penalty actions against persons under 12 U.S.C. § 1818(I) (see Civil Money Penalties Policy, PPM 5000-7, Revised, June 16, 1993); removal actions or personal cease and desist orders under 12 U.S.C. §§ 1818(e) or (b) against individuals; actions taken to enforce the various securities laws and regulations (see OCC's Securities Activities Enforcement Policy, PPM 5310-5 (October 6, 1988)); actions taken with respect to federal branches and agencies under the International Banking Act (see 12 U.S.C. § 3108); or actions under the International Lending and Supervision Act (see 12 U.S.C. § 3909).

B.   General Policy

When the OCC identifies safety and soundness or compliance problems in a national bank, the OCC works to achieve expeditious corrective and remedial action. The OCC uses a number of tools to carry out its supervisory responsibilities. These tools range from informal advice and moral suasion to formal enforcement and/or PCA and safety and soundness orders. Collectively, these will be referred to in this PPM as "corrective actions."

Effective bank supervision depends substantially on clear communications between the OCC and the bank followed by the bank's accomplishment of corrective measures. An OCC Report of Examination ("Report") must clearly identify and communicate the OCC's assessment of a bank's condition and describe any problems, concerns, weaknesses, or deficiencies as well as the primary cause of each. Once problems have been identified and communicated to the bank, the bank's senior management and board of directors will be expected to take appropriate corrective measures. In their communications with banks, examiners should specify, in priority order, those measures which are deemed necessary to correct problems and they should provide the bank with a realistic but firm timetable in which the bank must implement those measures. The actions a bank takes or agrees to take in response to its Report will be important factors in determining whether the OCC also should take corrective action and the severity of such action.

Section:	Bank Supervision	Subject:	Policy for Taking Corrective Action

Whenever possible, OCC corrective action should deal with weaknesses at an early stage, before they can develop into more serious problems. This may mean taking action well before problems are reflected in a bank's component or composite ratings. Corrective action may involve securing management and board commitments to undertake specific remedial measures to address the OCC's concerns. Once a bank has begun proper corrective actions to correct problems and prevent further deterioration, the OCC will follow up to ensure the success of such measures.

1.   Informal Supervisory and Enforcement Actions

A well-crafted Report that clearly identifies problems and puts the bank and its board on notice as to the need for corrective measures is a critical element of effective OCC supervision. While it is not expected that a Report will spell out every remedial measure necessary to address identified problems, a Report can and should provide clear guidance to the bank on what is expected.

A well-crafted and effectively communicated Report can also serve the same purpose that an informal enforcement action serves, i.e., to set out a blueprint for addressing problems and preventing them from becoming worse.

When it is necessary to go beyond the Report and obtain written commitments from a bank's management and board of directors to ensure that the problems identified in the Report will be corrected, the OCC may use informal enforcement actions. Informal enforcement actions can provide a bank with more explicit guidance and direction than is normally contained in a Report. Informal actions can also serve as evidence of the bank's commitment to correct identified problems before they affect the bank's condition.

Informal enforcement actions include: OCC-required board resolutions, commitment letters, memoranda of understanding, and other forms of written communication between the OCC and the bank intended to articulate and memorialize a bank's commitment to corrective measures to address safety and soundness and compliance concerns. Informal enforcement actions also include actions taken to withhold or condition corporate approvals, i.e., corporate leverage. (See Appendix A for a more complete description of informal enforcement actions.)

PPM 5310-3

POLICIES & PROCEDURES MANUAL

Comptroller of the Currency
Administrator of National Banks

Section: Bank Supervision   Subject: Policy for Taking Corrective Action

2.   Formal Supervisory and Enforcement Actions

The OCC has a wide variety of formal actions available to it to support its supervisory objectives. Formal actions are distinguishable from informal actions in that they are statutorily authorized (and in some cases mandated) and are generally more severe. They are employed when less formal remedial measures are considered inadequate, ineffective or otherwise unlikely to secure prompt correction of safety or soundness or compliance problems.

For purposes of this PPM, formal actions against a bank include: orders and formal written agreements within the meaning of 12 U.S.C. § 1818(b), capital directives under 12 U.S.C. § 3907, civil money penalties under 12 U.S.C. § 1818(I), conservatorships under 12 U.S.C. § 203 (see 12 U.S.C. § 1821(c)(5)), letters invoking conservatorship or receivership under 12 U.S.C. § 71a, any condition imposed in writing in connection with the granting of any corporate application within the meaning of 12 U.S.C. § 1818(b), mandatory and discretionary PCA measures under 12 U.S.C. § 1831o and safety and soundness orders under 12 U.S.C. § 1831p-1. Mandatory and discretionary PCA measures include the issuance of directives, reclassification actions, early resolution options, and all waivers, approvals, disapprovals, extensions, restrictions, limitations, exemptions or decisions permitted or otherwise required under 12 U.S.C. § 1831o and OCC's PCA regulations found in 12 CFR Part 6. (See Appendix A for a more complete description of formal enforcement actions, and Appendices B, C, D and E for a description of mandatory and discretionary actions under PCA.) (See also Banking Circular 268, Prompt Corrective Action, February 25, 1993).

Policy for Taking Corrective Action

A.   Selection of Corrective Actions

The OCC will make individual judgments as to the type of corrective action(s) appropriate for a given bank. The OCC will select the action or combination of actions best suited to address identified problems and effect remedial action. The policy that follows provides guidance to promote consistency for similar circumstances while preserving the flexibility to fashion the most appropriate form(s) of corrective action in response to specific circumstances. Generally, these actions will fall into one or more of the following categories:

Section: Bank Supervision   Subject: Policy for Taking Corrective Action

---

1. Formal and informal enforcement actions,

2. PCA measures (excluding reclassification actions),

3. Reclassification actions,

4. Orders requiring compliance with safety and soundness standards,

5. Early resolution.

B. Formal and Informal Enforcement Actions

The OCC will continue to rely primarily on informal or formal enforcement actions under 12 U.S.C. § 1818 or other forms of non-PCA measures to address supervisory concerns for banks that are "well-" or "adequately" capitalized under the OCC's PCA regulations. Accordingly, enforcement actions against these banks should normally be taken under Section 1818 or through use of other non-PCA measures (including capital directives under 12 U.S.C. § 3907).

PCA measures should only be used if non-PCA measures are considered to be inadequate to carry out the OCC's supervisory mission or PCA measures are uniquely suited to achieve the desired results in a particular case.

In some circumstances, the presumption for formal action under 12 U.S.C. § 1818 is particularly strong, even in the presence of a satisfactory composite CAMEL rating or compliance with capital adequacy standards under Parts 3 and 6. It is the OCC's policy that formal enforcement actions be taken whenever:

- The bank is experiencing **significant** problems in its systems, controls, internal audit programs, operating policies, methods of operations, or management information systems (i.e., operating in an unsafe or unsound manner), even if these problems have not yet resulted in a change of rating or been reflected in the bank's financial performance or condition;

POLICIES & PROCEDURES MANUAL

Comptroller of the Currency
Administrator of National Banks

Section: Bank Supervision   Subject: Policy for Taking Corrective Action

- There is significant insider abuse Ä whether or not the bank is immediately harmed;

- There are significant compliance problems or substantial violations of law;

- The bank or persons involved have disregarded or refused to respond to prior supervisory efforts to correct serious problems;

- The bank has failed or refused to satisfactorily maintain its books and records and as a result OCC examiners are unable to determine its true condition,

- There is substantial noncompliance or a lack of full compliance over an extended period of time either with commitments received in response to an OCC Report or with any enforcement action.

C.   PCA Measures

PCA measures are triggered by the capital levels set out in Part 6 to Title 12 of the Code of Federal Regulations. The OCC will consider using discretionary PCA measures whenever consistent with PCA's purpose, i.e., to "resolve the problems of problem institutions at the least possible long-term cost to the deposit insurance fund." For banks that are "undercapitalized," "significantly undercapitalized" or "critically undercapitalized" under Part 6 of OCC regulations, the OCC will consider using PCA measures prior to considering • 1818 enforcement. In particular, PCA measures may be appropriate in cases where the need for prompt action is present.

When an undercapitalized, significantly undercapitalized or critically undercapitalized bank is already subject to a formal enforcement action under • 1818, the OCC may elect to (1) keep the § 1818 document in place in its present form; (2) modify the document to reflect any additional requirements deemed necessary in view of the bank's capital category; (3) replace the document with a PCA Directive if PCA is considered a more effective supervisory measure; or (4) impose a PCA Directive while also maintaining a formal enforcement action against the bank. Whatever option the OCC chooses, additional mandatory PCA restrictions applicable to such banks will apply automatically.

Section:	Bank Supervision	Subject:	Policy for Taking Corrective Action

Section 1818 enforcement actions or other non-PCA measures for undercapitalized, significantly undercapitalized or critically undercapitalized banks will ordinarily not be pursued unless PCA is considered inadequate to carry out the OCC's supervisory objectives or non-PCA actions are determined to be uniquely suited to achieve the desired result.

D. Reclassification and More Severe Treatment

1. Introduction

The OCC may impose more severe limitations than a bank's PCA capital classification would otherwise permit or require if:

a. The OCC determines that the bank is in an unsafe or unsound condition or engaging in an unsafe or unsound practice; or

b. The OCC determines to apply corrective measures to undercapitalized or significantly undercapitalized banks otherwise only available under the next lower PCA category as "necessary to carry out the purposes of the Act."

2. Reclassification

If the OCC determines, after notice and opportunity for hearing (See 12 CFR § 19.221), that a bank is in an unsafe and unsound condition or is engaging in an unsafe or unsound practice, the OCC may:

a. reclassify a well-capitalized bank as an adequately capitalized bank;

b. require an adequately capitalized bank to comply with one or more requirements applicable to an undercapitalized bank; or

c. require an undercapitalized bank to take one or more actions applicable to significantly undercapitalized banks.

POLICIES & PROCEDURES MANUAL

Comptroller of the Currency
Administrator of National Banks

Section: Bank Supervision   Subject: Policy for Taking Corrective Action

3.   More Severe Treatment

The OCC also may apply corrective measures to undercapitalized or significantly undercapitalized banks otherwise only available under the next lower PCA category if the OCC determines that such measures are "necessary to carry out the purposes of the Act." (See 12 U.S.C. §§ 1831o(e)(5) and (f)(5)). For example, the OCC could apply more severe provisions to undercapitalized banks normally applicable only to significantly undercapitalized banks if it determined that these provisions would better serve the purposes of PCA. This type of action is discretionary and does not require a hearing.

The OCC will use its reclassification authority and its authority to apply more severe treatment only when:

      a.   reclassification or more severe treatment is clearly permitted by law; and

      b.   reclassification or more severe treatment is expected to correct an unsafe or unsound practice or condition consistent with the purposes of PCA; or

      c.   enforcement remedies under 12 U.S.C. § 1818 are considered inadequate to deal successfully with the bank's problems in a timely manner; or

      d.   reclassification or more severe treatment is considered necessary to permit the OCC to exercise one or more forms of corrective action otherwise unavailable to the OCC under 12 U.S.C. § 1818.

The OCC will review carefully all recommendations for reclassification or more severe treatment to ensure that their use is consistent with the policy set forth above.

Comptroller of the Currency
Administrator of National Banks

Section: Bank Supervision   Subject: Policy for Taking Corrective Action

---

E.   Orders Requiring Compliance with Safety and Soundness Standards

Under 12 U.S.C. § 1831p-1, a bank that fails to comply with any established safety and soundness standard must file a plan to correct the deficiency with the OCC and the OCC must approve the plan. (Final regulations will become effective in December 1993 setting forth applicable safety and soundness standards under this provision of law.) If the bank does not file a plan or fails to satisfactorily implement it, the OCC must issue an order requiring the bank to correct the deficiency. The OCC may also order the bank to take any additional action that the OCC determines will better carry out the purposes of 12 U.S.C. § 1831p-1. The OCC must also take additional action against a bank that has not corrected a deficiency if the bank has experienced either extraordinary growth or a change in control.

Twelve U.S.C. § 1831p-1 is designed to ensure that the OCC requires banks to address weaknesses in their operations other than lack of adequate capital. The OCC would be in compliance with this requirement if it already had imposed an enforcement action addressing the deficiency when the bank failed to meet a 12 U.S.C. § 1831p-1 safety and soundness standard.

Accordingly, corrective actions under 12 U.S.C. § 1831p-1 should be used to address a bank's failure to meet a safety and soundness standard only if that deficiency is not already the subject of an enforcement action and the bank is otherwise "well-" or "adequately" capitalized.

F.   Early Resolution

The OCC also has the authority to place a bank into receivership, conservatorship, or to require its sale or merger while the bank still has equity capital of more than 2 percent if such action would help resolve a problem at the least long-term cost to the Bank Insurance Fund. Early resolution can reduce or limit losses that might otherwise result if the bank is allowed to remain open until its capital has dropped below 2 percent or has been exhausted. Early resolution can be considered, for example, when a bank is: losing capital, has no realistic prospects for recapitalization, or is engaging in practices likely to increase losses in the future. Once the bank's capital has dropped below 2 percent, the provisions of 12 U.S.C. § 1831o(h) operate to expose the bank to all restrictions and limitations applicable to critically undercapitalized banks, including the provisions of § 1821o(h)(3) requiring that the bank be placed into receivership or conservatorship.

| Section: | Bank Supervision | Subject: | Policy for Taking Corrective Action |

Supervisory offices should develop an early resolution contingency plan involving a merger, sale, conservatorship or receivership when a bank becomes undercapitalized. They should consider the point beyond which additional enforcement or PCA is not likely to prevent failure or reduce the costs associated with it. Once a decision is made to adopt an early resolution approach, OCC resources should be focused on the best available alternative at the least cost to the Bank Insurance Fund. All OCC offices involved in early resolution planning (e.g., those offices exercising bank supervision or corporate licensing functions) should be apprised of the possible need to take steps to support early resolution.

G.   Determining Severity of Corrective Actions

1.   Introduction

The selection of specific corrective measures should be tailored to the institution and designed to correct identified deficiencies, improve its overall condition and generally return the bank to a safe and sound condition as soon as possible. The severity of the corrective measures utilized should be based primarily on two factors: the bank's condition and the OCC's assessment as to the degree of cooperation, responsiveness and overall capability displayed by the bank's management and board.

2.   1-Rated and 2-Rated Banks

For bank's with a composite rating of 1 or 2, examiners and the supervisory office should obtain affirmative commitments for corrective action from the bank's senior management, the board of directors, and where appropriate, ownership. This includes commitments to address problems identified in an OCC Report relating to the bank's systems, controls, internal audit programs, operating policies and methods of operations, and/or management information systems. Such commitments need not take the form of an enforcement action if the examiner and supervisory office consider other measures (e.g., oral assurances, correspondence, or action taken or promised) adequate to address OCC criticisms.

Section:	Bank Supervision	Subject:	Policy for Taking Corrective Action

Decisions to take stronger action will be the responsibility of the supervisory office. The supervisory office will consider the seriousness of the deficiency and the commitment and ability of the bank's management and board to correct deficiencies. When confidence in the board or management is low, OCC corrective measures should increase in scope and severity.

3.   3-Rated Banks

When considering corrective measures on a 3-rated bank, the supervisory office will analyze the overall condition of and outlook for the bank, its record of compliance with previous criticisms or supervisory actions and the OCC's degree of confidence in the ability of the bank's management and board to correct all identified deficiencies and return the bank to a safe and sound condition.

Since the OCC's assessment of the ability of the bank's management, board, or ownership to correct the problems is key, a 3-rated bank with strong management could be considered for informal action or no action if other circumstances suggest that the remedial measures necessary to restore the bank to a safe and sound condition are present. If an enforcement action is used on this type of 3-rated bank, the corrective measures would likely be less severe.

A 3-rated bank with weak management should be considered for a formal enforcement action or PCA (if appropriate). The corrective measures should be appropriately severe and should address explicitly how the measures are to be carried out.

4.   4-Rated and 5-Rated Banks

A strong presumption exists to take formal corrective measures whenever a bank receives a composite rating of 4 or 5. As in 3-rated banks, the capability, cooperation, integrity and commitment of the bank's management, its board of directors or ownership to correct the problems are key. Because a 4- or 5-rated bank is more likely to fail, however, a formal OCC corrective action is presumed necessary.

POLICIES & PROCEDURES MANUAL

Comptroller of the Currency
Administrator of National Banks

Section: Bank Supervision   Subject: Policy for Taking Corrective Action

For 4-rated banks currently subject only to informal enforcement actions, the supervisory office must consider imposing a formal enforcement action when the bank's rating is reaffirmed or downgraded to a 5 rating. Similarly, the supervisory office must also consider imposing formal enforcement actions against a 5-rated bank when the office has reaffirmed the rating. A recommendation to maintain an informal action in lieu of a formal action must be supported by the appropriate Supervision Review Committee (SRC) in accordance with the procedures set out below.

Also, the supervisory office will presume that any enforcement action taken against a 4- or 5-rated bank can only be maintained or strengthened until such time as that bank's rating is no longer a 4 or 5. The SRC must address and make recommendations regarding decisions to modify, terminate or reduce the severity of existing enforcement actions, as well as the content of any new enforcement action on all 4- and 5-rated banks.

Procedures for All Corrective Actions

A.   Procedures

Each office or person responsible for corrective actions will establish procedures to apply corrective actions promptly, fairly and consistently. A copy of each office's written procedures must be forwarded to the senior deputy comptroller for Bank Supervision Operations.

The senior deputy comptroller for Bank Supervision Operations will appoint a Washington Supervision Review Committee (WSRC) and each district deputy comptroller will appoint a District Supervision Review Committee (DSRC). Each SRC will consider supervisory remedies, PCA measures, enforcement actions, and safety and soundness orders in conjunction with the OCC's supervisory strategy for the bank and OCC policy and recommend appropriate action to the senior deputy comptroller for Bank Supervision Operations or the district deputy comptroller, as appropriate.

The DSRC or WSRC, as appropriate, will make recommendations for decisions on all formal enforcement actions, any action against a 4- or 5-rated bank, any exceptions to policy and any actions involving use of OCC's PCA authority or safety and soundness orders.

POLICIES & PROCEDURES MANUAL

Comptroller of the Currency
Administrator of National Banks

Section: Bank Supervision   Subject: Policy for Taking Corrective Action

Once a year, the WSRC and each DSRC, respectively, will review their operational procedures and membership. They will submit proposed changes to the senior deputy comptroller for Bank Supervision Operations or district deputy comptroller, as appropriate.

B.   Support for Decisions

The examiner and supervisory office must document in writing decisions on whether or not to proceed with an enforcement action or PCA directive and the nature and severity of the action. Those responsible will also ensure that decisions are recorded in the OCC's Supervisory Monitoring System (SMS).

C.   Timeliness of Corrective Actions

The OCC will process and take corrective actions as soon as practical once an examiner or supervisory office has identified and documented a need for such action. When circumstances warrant, the supervisory office may take appropriate action during an examination. Actions should be taken within the following maximum time periods whenever possible.

Within 15 calendar days following:

1.   a final decision to change or retain a 3-, 4-, or 5-rated bank's composite rating,

2.   a decision to downgrade any bank's rating to a 3, 4 or 5,

3.   a determination that a bank is significantly or critically undercapitalized,

4.   a determination that an undercapitalized bank has failed to submit an acceptable capital plan or has failed in some material respect to implement it, or

5.   a determination that a bank has violated a safety and soundness standard.

Comptroller of the Currency
Administrator of National Banks

Section: Bank Supervision   Subject: Policy for Taking Corrective Action

The supervisory office must decide whether to proceed with an appropriate corrective action or to change (upgrade or downgrade) an existing corrective action.

For delegated actions, the DSRC must decide on the form and content of any such action within 30 calendar days following the decision to proceed with or change the action.

For nondelegated actions, the WSRC must act on the recommendation of the DSRC, Special Supervision (SPSU) or Multinational Banking (MNB) as to the form and content of the proposed action or change within 30 calendar days after receiving a recommendation from the DSRC, SPSU or MNB.

Within 15 days following the SRC decision, the supervisory office must provide documents relating to the proposed action to the bank's board of directors or its duly authorized representative. The supervisory office must arrange a date for a board meeting for execution of the document, preferably within 30 days of the board's receipt of the documents. The supervisory office will document any exceptions to the time frames for action set out in this policy.

D.   Content of Corrective Action Documents

Corrective action documents should address substantive supervisory problems. Such actions need not address every supervisory issue identified. Each action, however, should clearly list any prohibited or restricted activities and, where appropriate, prioritize remedial measures to be taken, and the time in which the bank, its board of directors or management must act. Corrective action documents should also explicitly state what action is expected of those parties subject to the document.

Wherever feasible the relevant document should address the problems and causes of the problems identified in the Report. Examiners and the supervisory office should clearly distinguish serious problems warranting immediate attention and lesser problems that the bank can defer until the priority problems are resolved.

While the language in corrective action documents may be similar from one bank to another, the supervisory office should tailor specific remedial action for each individual bank.

E.   OCC Responsibilities Following Taking of Corrective Actions

The memorandum supporting a decision whether or not to proceed with or revise a corrective action document must include a clear statement describing future OCC action. If a decision is made to proceed with a corrective action, the memorandum must describe the time frames in which the OCC will monitor compliance with the action. The OCC follow-up will be determined by the time frames in the document. At a minimum, the statement must address the timing and scope of the next examination.

The examiner should also provide a description of and timing for further OCC action after the OCC has reviewed bank compliance with the document. The description should address the scope and timing of any proposed follow-up, including examinations or visits to the bank, as well as any proposed meetings with management and the board and any additional actions recommended.

In cases of substantial noncompliance with a corrective action document, the examiner or supervisory office will consider recommending civil money penalties (if appropriate) or imposing additional restrictions on the bank, its management or the board of directors.

F.   Termination or Modification of Corrective Actions

The supervisory office may terminate or modify a corrective action document whenever it believes that such action is consistent with the OCC's supervisory objectives for the bank. The supervisory office must document the improved or improving condition of the bank together with the bank's substantial compliance with the action to support a decision to terminate or modify a corrective action document. The supervisory office must also ensure that this decision is entered into entries into the OCC's Supervisory Monitoring System (SMS).

POLICIES & PROCEDURES MANUAL

Comptroller of the Currency
Administrator of National Banks

Section: Bank Supervision   Subject: Policy for Taking Corrective Action

Public Disclosure of Corrective Actions

A.   Disclosure Required by Law

The OCC is required by 12 U.S.C. § 1818(u) to disclose publicly certain types of agency actions. The OCC must disclose publicly all final orders entered into pursuant to 12 U.S.C. § 1818(b), civil money penalties (including those for late or inaccurate call reports), removal orders, capital directives, and any modification and/or termination of such actions. The OCC must also disclose publicly all formal agreements under 12 U.S.C. § 1818(b), and any conditions imposed in writing in connection with an application which are enforceable under section 1818(b). The OCC must also disclose any final PCA directives, reclassifications under 12 U.S.C. § 1831o(g) or safety and soundness orders issued pursuant to 12 U.S.C. § 1831p-1(e).

The OCC is not required to disclose publicly temporary cease and desist orders, conservatorships or receiverships. There is also no requirement for the OCC to disclose informal actions, i.e., memoranda of understanding, commitment letters, or board resolutions.

Under certain limited circumstances, the OCC may delay mandatory public disclosure for a reasonable period of time.

Once a month, the OCC's Communications Division will publish a list of formal enforcement actions and final PCA directives that includes the name of the person or bank involved, the type of action, the date of the action, and whether the board of directors consented to the action. The Communications Division will maintain a file of all final formal enforcement actions and will provide copies of these documents upon request.

B.   Discretionary OCC Disclosure

The OCC will consider public disclosures beyond those required by law on a case-by-case basis (e.g., matters that the OCC believes would be in the public interest to disclose).

The OCC will publicly disclose enforcement actions taken to remedy violations of the federal securities laws and/or related OCC regulations in accordance with provisions of PPM 5310-5, which sets out the Securities Activities Enforcement Policy.

POLICIES & PROCEDURES MANUAL

Comptroller of the Currency
Administrator of National Banks

Section: Bank Supervision   Subject: Policy for Taking Corrective Action

C.   Requirements for Disclosures by National Banks

Disclosures described in paragraphs A. and B. above refer only to OCC's required or discretionary disclosures. Nothing in either paragraph is intended to relieve any national bank, or, where applicable, its holding company, of its independent obligations to make required disclosures under the various securities laws and related regulations.

Responsibilities

The senior deputy comptroller for Bank Supervision Operations has the primary responsibility to use the OCC's enforcement authority under 12 U.S.C. § 1818, PCA authority under 12 U.S.C. § 1831o and safety and soundness authority under 12 U.S.C. § 1831p-1 as necessary to accomplish the OCC's supervisory objectives and may delegate this authority to initiate, negotiate, execute, modify and terminate enforcement actions covered by this PPM. Any authority delegated by the senior deputy comptroller for Bank Supervision Operations may not be sub-delegated without the senior deputy's express written approval.

Stephen R. Steinbrink
Senior Deputy Comptroller for
Bank Supervision Operations

Appendix C

Prior Approval of Dividends

If prior approval of a dividend is required under either 12 USC 60 or from an administrative action, the OCC considers the same factors. The OCC generally would deny a request by a bank to pay a dividend to protect the market perception of its stock. Examiners must review such situations carefully to determine if failure to pay the dividend could seriously impair the bank's prospects for recovery.

The OCC is flexible in granting prior approval for payment of dividends subject to 12 USC 60(b) constraints. OCC supervisory offices may grant prior approval to national banks' requests to pay dividends in advance of the period(s) in which the dividend(s) would be declared. This advance approval may cover several anticipated dividend payments, provided that the bank projects sufficient current net income during those periods to support the amount of the dividends declared.

This policy applies only to the timing of the OCC's approval of dividends subject to the prior approval requirements of 12 USC 60(b). It does not exempt national banks from complying with this law. Advance approvals will not apply to any proposed dividend payments that are in excess of the current period net income for national banks that are otherwise subject to the constraints of 12 USC 60(b). Further, this policy does not apply to those national banks that fail to meet other statutory dividend requirements, such as those contained in 12 USC 56 and in 12 USC 1831o.

Prior to initiating such a request, a national bank should ensure that it has prepared and analyzed sufficient information. Both the national bank and the OCC supervisory office should consider:

- The reasonableness of the bank's request, including its historical dividend payout ratio and projected dividend payments.

- The bank's historical trends and current projections for capital growth through earnings retention.

- The overall condition of the institution, with particular emphasis on current and projected capital adequacy.

- The reason(s) for which the bank became subject to the restrictions of 12 USC 60(b).

- Any other information that the supervisory office deems pertinent to reviewing the bank's request.

The supervisory office may take one of the following actions based upon its review of the bank's request:

- Approve it without further restrictions.

- Approve it subject to certain conditions.

- Deny the request.

In applicable cases, the national bank is responsible for requesting advance approval and submitting documentation supporting it. The appropriate OCC supervisory office will not grant an advance approval for dividend payments independent of a national bank's request or without sufficient review of the facts.

The examiner or appropriate OCC official should consider approving dividend requests using the following criteria:

- Compliance with applicable laws and regulations — Check for compliance with 12 USC 56 and 60. The request must be denied, if the dividend would violate 12 USC 56.

- Preferred stock dividends are subject to the restrictions of 12 USC 60, but they are not subject to 12 USC 56. If a proposed common or preferred dividend would exceed the restrictions outlined in 12 USC 60, the examiner analyzing a dividend request should give particular attention to the issues of capital adequacy and quality of earnings.

- Compliance with the minimum capital requirements — Review the effect from the proposed common or preferred dividend on the bank's capital requirements established by 12 CFR 3. If the bank's capital base is already below the minimum required, or if the dividend would cause the bank to drop below the minimum, the OCC should deny the dividend request as an unsafe and unsound banking practice. The examiner's analysis of a dividend request must go beyond merely determining technical compliance with minimum capital requirements. The examiner should also assess the result of the proposed dividend on the bank's projected future capital adequacy.

- Banks subject to administrative actions — If a bank is operating under an administrative action that requires it to maintain a level of capital higher than the regulatory minimums, the OCC should deny any dividend that would cause the bank's capital to decline below that level. If the OCC approves such a dividend, the examiner must detail fully the extenuating circumstances in SMS.

- Purpose of the dividend — One must examine the reasons the bank has decided to pay the dividend. The bank should support dividends with its income. If the dividend is necessary for debt service, the examiner should consider whether the bank planned to pay a dividend for that purpose. If not, the need for dividends may signal potential weaknesses in the owner's financial condition. The shareholders also may need the dividend to fund other operations, such as in a holding company. The OCC generally will deny excessive or unwarranted dividend requests to meet stockholders' debt service requirements. However, some banks with more than adequate capital may request an excess dividend to reduce debt. If after reviewing the bank's request and other documentation the supervisory office determines there is no supervisory concern, the OCC will generally approve the request.

- Consistency with projections, capital plan, and strategic plan — The proposed dividend should be consistent with the bank's projections, capital plan, and strategic plan. If the dividend is consistent with the bank's stated plans, the examiner must consider whether those plans and projections are still appropriate given the bank's present circumstances. If they are not, the examiner should ask the bank to make appropriate adjustments and should incorporate the updated information into the analysis of the dividend request.

- Earnings — In assessing a request from an institution for approval of an exception to 12 USC 60, the examiner should consider both the bank's earnings trends and the quality of its earnings. If the bank has proposed a dividend even though it recorded a net loss, the examiner must evaluate whether that performance represents a short-term impairment of the bank's earnings or signals a sustained downward trend.

Processing Requests

The supervisory office should attempt to respond to all dividend requests within 30 days of receipt of the request. If additional information is needed to make the decision, the supervisory office should advise the bank in writing within 15 days of receiving the request. If a response is not possible within 30 days, the supervisory office should inform the bank in writing of the reason.

The examiner analyzing a dividend request should enter into SMS a narrative record of the analysis as an "Other Significant Event" (OSE), using the title "Dividend Request." The record should address each of the points previously discussed and include all other relevant information. If the OCC takes any action that contradicts that guidance, the examiner should document thoroughly the extenuating circumstances and the justification. When the narrative record is maintained in the bank file, the examiner must enter a summary of the decision into SMS.

A bank occasionally may request the OCC's approval of a dividend without being required to do so. In those cases, the supervisory office should determine whether it wishes to provide a formal response.

Appendix D

Guarantee of CRP by Controlling Company

The OCC will not approve any CRP unless each company controlling the bank submits a written guarantee of the plan. The guarantee is intended for the holding company to provide a financial commitment and appropriate assurances of performance to the OCC that the company's subsidiary bank will comply with the bank's CRP.

The company's aggregate liability under the guarantee is limited to the lesser of:

1. Five percent of the bank's total assets at the time the bank was notified or deemed to have notice that it was undercapitalized, or

2. the amount necessary to restore the capital of the bank to the levels required for the institution to be adequately capitalized, as those levels were defined at the time the bank initially failed to comply with its CRP.

Duration of Guarantee

The guarantee and limit of liability for performance of a capital restoration plan expires after the OCC notifies the national bank in writing that it has remained adequately capitalized for four consecutive calendar quarters (See 12 CFR 6.5(I)(1)(ii)). This will permit the OCC and the bank to verify that the guarantee has expired.

Additional Guarantees

The OCC's regulation at 12 CFR 6.5(I)(1)(ii) provides that the expiration of a guarantee given by a company or fulfillment of a guarantee given by a company in connection with one CRP does not relieve the company from the obligation to guarantee another CRP that may be required at a future date for the same bank if it again becomes undercapitalized. Fulfillment of one guarantee up to the statutory limit would not reduce the amount of any guarantee of a future CRP for the same bank.

In addition, a new or revised guarantee is required if the bank is required to submit a new or revised CRP pursuant to 12 CFR 6.5(a)(2). Section 6.5(a)(2) provides that a bank that has submitted and is operating under an approved CRP must submit an additional CRP when it falls into a lower capital category if the OCC notifies the bank that it must submit a new or revised CRP.

Collection of Guarantee

Each company controlling a given bank is jointly and severally liable for the guarantee. The OCC may direct the bank to seek payment of the full amount of the guarantee from any and all the companies issuing the guarantee.

Failure to Perform Guarantee

Failure by the company to perform fully its guarantee will constitute a material failure to implement the bank's capital restoration plan and will subject the bank to the provisions of 12 USC 1831o(f)(1)(B)(ii) applicable to banks that have failed to implement a capital restoration plan. In addition, the bank may be subject to enforcement actions pursuant to 12 USC 1818, including civil money penalties, for failure to comply with an OCC regulation.

The OCC supervisory office may consult with the Federal Reserve analyst at the appropriate Federal Reserve bank to discuss provisions of the guarantee. The OCC supervisory office will determine on a case-by-case basis the adequacy of such guarantees and assurances of performance.

Pledge of Holding Company Assets May Be Required

Section 1831o(e)(2)(C)(ii)(II) states that the holding company must provide "appropriate assurances of performance" to satisfy the guarantee requirement. These assurances will vary on a case-by-case basis depending on the bank's condition and willingness to implement changes, the strength of the holding company, and other relevant factors. In the case of a cooperative, strong holding company controlling an undercapitalized bank, the OCC generally will accept a bank's CRP if it includes a written guarantee from the company with a copy of its audited financial statements.

In other cases, the OCC may require a pledge of certain nonbanking assets. For example, the OCC may require a financially weak holding company that controls an undercapitalized bank to pledge assets to secure its guarantee. Similarly, a holding company that controls a significantly or critically undercapitalized bank generally will be expected to include a contractual pledge of assets regardless of financial strength. A security agreement and a UCC-1 financing statement may also be expected, when collateral is pledged, to secure the holding company's guarantee before the OCC accepts the bank's CRP.

In addition, if the pledged assets are not of a type that a national bank can legally hold, the pledge agreement should provide that the assets will be liquidated within six months of being contributed to the bank.

The need for a pledge also depends on the organizational structure of the holding company. In a multi-tiered holding company, each company is jointly and severally liable for implementing the bank's capital restoration plans. For the OCC to accept a bank's CRP, each company must guarantee the CRP and provide adequate assurances of performance. Intermediate shell holding companies may, however, rely on the financial resources of the parent company or of a third party as adequate assurance of performance on the guarantee.

For a shell holding company or a company that has limited resources the OCC will require a guarantee to consider the bank's CRP. Given the company's lack of resources, however, a pledge of assets generally will not be required. Instead, the OCC will evaluate the CRP on the same basis that it evaluates plans submitted by banks owned by individuals. If the OCC would approve a CRP submitted by a bank owned by an individual, it will approve a similar CRP submitted by a bank owned by a shell holding company.

Request for Legal Opinion

The OCC may also request that the bank and the company obtain a legal opinion from the bank holding company's counsel that the guarantee and any pledge of assets securing such guarantee, if applicable, constitutes a legally binding commitment against the holding company that is given in the ordinary course of business for adequate consideration.

Interagency Coordination

In evaluating a holding company guarantee, the OCC may consult with the appropriate Federal Reserve Bank on the condition of the holding company and its ability to fulfill its guarantee. The OCC may also consult with the FDIC on the terms of the guarantee to ensure that the FDIC's interest as receiver would be protected if the bank is later placed in receivership.

Approval on Case-by-Case Basis

The appropriate OCC supervisory office will determine on a case-by-case basis the adequacy of any guarantee and assurances of performance by a controlling company.

Appendix E

Sample Capital Restoration Plan Guarantee

The sample guarantee:

- References the parties to the guarantee (the bank and the guarantor holding company(s)).

- Incorporates by reference the capital restoration plan submitted for approval by the bank.

- Provides that the holding company unconditionally guarantees and provides a financial commitment that the bank will comply with its CRP.

- Provides that the holding company will (1) take any action directly required under the CRP; (2) take any corporate actions necessary to enable the bank to take actions required of the bank under the CRP; (3) not take any action that would impede the bank's ability to implement its CRP; (4) ensure that the bank is staffed by competent management; and (5) restrict transactions between the holding company and the bank.

- States the limit of liability and the promise to pay the amount described.

- Incorporates by reference a certified resolution of the board of directors of the holding company regarding the guarantee.

- Describes the consideration provided and certain rights of the parties.

- Provides for the pledge of holding company assets, or other appropriate collateral, to secure the guarantee, when deemed appropriate.

- Includes certain other provisions, such as a statement on governing law.

The guarantee is patterned after a standard commercial guarantee. It requires the controlling company to perform on its guarantee when the bank notifies the company that the bank has failed to comply with its CRP. If the bank declines or delays in enforcing the guarantee, the OCC may take action directing the bank to enforce the guarantee or take any other action under PCA or 12 U.S.C. 1818 as may be appropriate. In the event the bank is placed in receivership, the FDIC as receiver would be entitled to the proceeds of any contribution by the company.

Capital Restoration Plan Guaranty Agreement

This Agreement is made this _____ day of _____, 19__, by and between [First National Bank, Any Town, State], a national banking association chartered and examined by the Office of the Comptroller of the Currency ("Comptroller") pursuant to the National Bank Act of

1864, as amended, 12 U.S.C. § 1 et seq., (the "Bank") and [First Bankholding Corporation, Inc.], a "controlling company" that controls the Bank for purposes of 12 U.S.C. § 1831o and 12 CFR Part 6, (the "Guarantor").

WHEREAS, the Bank is [undercapitalized, significantly undercapitalized, critically undercapitalized] pursuant to 12 U.S.C. § 1831o and 12 CFR Part 6. The Bank was notified, or was deemed to have notice, in accordance with 12 CFR 6.3, that it is [undercapitalized, significantly undercapitalized, critically undercapitalized] on [Date].

WHEREAS, the Bank has submitted a capital restoration plan ("CRP") in accordance with 12 U.S.C. § 1831o(e). The CRP is attached as Exhibit A and incorporated herein by reference.

WHEREAS, the Bank desires to obtain the Guarantor's guaranty that the Bank will comply with the CRP to obtain approval of the CRP from the Comptroller;

WHEREAS, the Guarantor desires to guarantee the Bank's performance of the CRP and to provide assurances of performance.

WHEREAS, the Guarantor represents that it owns and controls 100% of the stock of the Bank and expects to derive advantage from its guaranty by enhancing the financial strength of the Guarantor and the value to its shareholders by enhancing the financial strength of its asset, the Bank;

NOW THEREFORE, in consideration of the representations set forth above, the parties agree as follows:

1. Guaranty. The Guarantor(s) [jointly and severally] unconditionally guarantee(s) that the Bank will comply with the CRP until the Comptroller notifies the Bank, in writing, that the Bank has been "adequately capitalized", in accordance with 12 CFR 6.4, on average for four consecutive quarters.

2. Additional Undertakings by Guarantor. The Guarantor shall use its best efforts to:
    (a)   take any actions directly required of the holding company under the CRP;
    (b)   take any corporate actions necessary to enable the Bank to take actions required of the Bank under the CRP;
    (c)   not take any action that would impede the Bank's ability to implement its CRP;
    (d)   ensure that the Bank is staffed by competent management; and
    (e)   restrict transactions between the Guarantor and the Bank as provided in 12 CFR Part 6.

3. Performance of Guaranty. Upon receipt of written notice from the Comptroller that the Bank has failed to comply with the CRP, the Bank shall notify the Guarantor in writing of its failure to comply with the CRP and the Guarantor shall pay to the Bank, or its successors or assigns, the amount indicated in the Bank's notice as necessary to bring the Bank into compliance with the CRP. The amount indicated in the Bank's notice to the Guarantor shall be the amount indicated in the Comptroller's notice to the Bank. Notwithstanding the foregoing, the Guarantor's total liability under this Agreement shall not exceed 5 percent of the Bank's total assets at the time the Bank was notified, in accordance with 12 CFR 6.3, that the Bank was [undercapitalized, significantly undercapitalized, or critically undercapitalized] or the amount necessary to bring the Bank into compliance with all capital standards applicable to the Bank at the time the Bank failed to so comply.

4. Grant of Security Interest. To secure its performance under this Agreement and to provide adequate assurance of performance, as required under 12 U.S.C. § 1831o, the Guarantor has entered into a security agreement pledging certain specified assets of the Guarantor on behalf of the Bank. The Security Agreement is attached hereto as Exhibit B and incorporated herein by reference.

5. Authority of Guarantor. The Board of Directors of the Guarantor have entered into a resolution ("Resolution") certifying that the Guarantor is authorized to enter into this Agreement. A certified copy of the Resolution is attached hereto as Exhibit C and incorporated herein by reference.

6. Miscellaneous.
    A. Legally Binding, Enforceable Commitment. The parties agree that the Agreement is a binding and enforceable contractual commitment.
    B. Conservatorship or Receivership of the Bank. This Agreement shall survive the appointment of a conservator or receiver for the Bank, and shall continue as a binding contractual commitment of the Guarantor, its successors and assigns.
    C. Governing Laws. This Agreement and the rights and obligations hereunder shall be governed by and shall be construed in accordance with the Federal law of the United States, and, in the absence of controlling Federal law, in accordance with the laws of the [state where the Guarantor is incorporated] [State of New York].
    D. No Waiver. No failure or delay on the part of the Bank in the exercise of any right or remedy shall operate as a waiver or forbearance thereof, nor shall any partial exercise of any right or remedy preclude other or further exercise of any other right or remedy.
    E. Fees and Expenses. The Guarantor shall pay any attorneys' fees and other reasonable expenses incurred by the Bank in exercising its rights or seeking any remedies hereunder.
    F. Severability. In the event any one or more of the provisions contained herein should be held invalid, illegal or unenforceable in any respect, the validity, legality and enforceability of the remaining provisions contained herein shall not in any way be affected or impaired thereby. The parties shall endeavor in good faith negotiations to replace the invalid, illegal or unenforceable provisions with valid provisions the economic effect of which comes as close as possible to that of the invalid, illegal or unenforceable provisions.
    G. No Oral Change. This Agreement may not be modified, amended, changed, discharged or terminated orally, but may be done so only by an agreement and signed by the party against whom the enforcement of the modification, amendment, change, discharge or termination is sought.
    H. Multiple Guarantors. The Bank may, in its discretion, enforce this Agreement against any and all Guarantors.
    I. Modification. This Agreement (and the accompanying Security Agreement, if any) reflects the complete and full agreement entered among the parties and may not be modified, released, renewed or extended in any manner except by a writing signed by all the parties and unless such modification is approved by the OCC in writing.

J. Authority to Execute. Each of the undersigned warrant that he or she is duly authorized to execute the Agreement and to bind the parties to the Agreement. Each of the undersigned acknowledges that this Agreement is binding without reference to whether it is signed by any other person or persons.

K. Addresses for Notice. Any notice hereunder shall be in writing and shall be delivered by hand or sent by United States express mail or commercial express mail, postage prepaid, and addressed as follows:

If to the Bank:

If to the Guarantor:

IN WITNESS WHEREOF, the parties hereto have duly executed this Agreement as of the day and year first above written.

_____By: _____
Bank   Name and Title
_____By: _____
Guarantor   Name and Title

FUNDS FLOW ANALYSIS
OF THE ABC BANK (CONSOLIDATED COMPANY)
FOR SELECTED ASSETS AND CREDIT SENSITIVE LIABILITIES
$ Thousands

Sample format, tailor as appropriate.

	BANK ASSETS				BANK LIABILITIES						PARENT NONBANK ASSETS	NONBANK LIABILITIES
Quarter	(1) Federal Reserve Balance	(2) Total Loans & Leases	(3) Free Securities	(4) Money Market Assets	(5) DDA Net of Float	(6) Consumer Deposits	(7) Fed Funds Purchased	(8) CDs > $100M	(10) Foreign Deposits	(9) Other Sensitive Funds/Dep	(11) Short-Term Assets	(12) Short-Term Liabs
1	$5,000	$310,000	$70,000	$7,500	$98,000	$389,000	$10,000	$40,350	$0	$0	$10,000	$8,500
2	$5,000	$320,000	$68,000	$7,500	$94,000	$384,000	$10,000	$42,000	$1,000	$1,000	$10,000	$8,500
3	$5,200	$325,000	$66,500	$6,800	$94,000	$383,000	$12,000	$43,000	$1,000	$2,200	$10,000	$8,500
4	$5,100	$330,000	$67,500	$5,500	$92,400	$384,000	$14,500	$44,000	$1,000	$3,800	$10,000	$8,500
5	$5,000	$345,000	$68,000	$5,000	$90,400	$383,900	$13,000	$47,400	$1,000	$4,000	$10,000	$8,500
6	$4,800	$396,000	$23,200	$5,000	$74,000	$377,000	$10,000	$50,500	$1,000	$5,500	$10,000	$8,500
7	$5,100	$455,500	$19,000	$4,000	$75,300	$370,000	$11,000	$51,000	$2,700	$7,500	$6,000	$4,500
8	$3,900	$473,000	$12,500	$2,000	$80,000	$365,000	$14,000	$51,100	$5,000	$10,400	$4,500	$3,000
Change from previous period	($1,200)	$17,500	($6,500)	($2,000)	$4,700	($5,000)	$3,000	$100	$2,300	$2,900	($1,500)	($1,500)

Sources and Uses - Quarter 7 to Quarter 8			
Sources		**Uses**	
FRB BALANCE	$1,200	LOANS & LEASES	$17,500
FREE SECURITIES	$6,500	CONSUMER DEP	$5,000
MMA	$2,000		
DDA	$4,700		$22,500
FFP	$3,000		
CDs	$100		
FOREIGN DEP	$2,300		
OTHER LIABS	$2,900		
	$22,700		

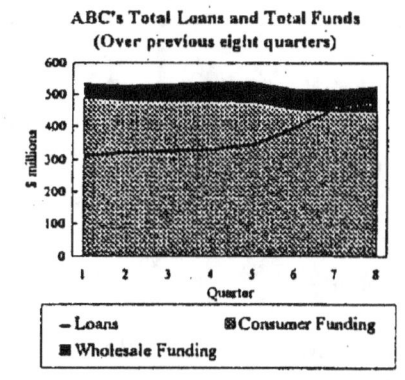

ABC's Total Loans and Total Funds (Over previous eight quarters)

— Loans ▨ Consumer Funding ■ Wholesale Funding

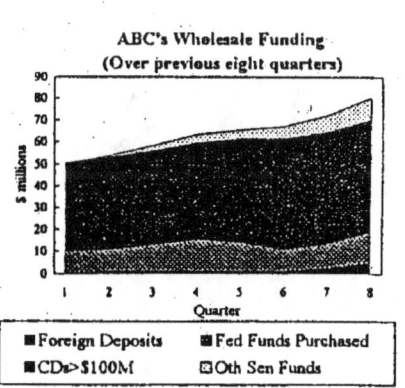

ABC's Wholesale Funding (Over previous eight quarters)

■ Foreign Deposits ■ Fed Funds Purchased ■ CDs>$100M ▨ Oth Sen Funds

NOTE: Sources and uses do not balance on this schedule since it purposely includes only balance sheet line items likely to affect liquidity. Longer term assets/liabilities, such as fixed assets or other liabilities, which usually have little impact on liquidity, are excluded in order to focus on meaningful cash flows. The out of balance condition can be monitored and controlled, and if significant should be researched. This process allows for a more timely availability and presentation of data.

Appendix F - Continued

Funds Flow Analysis Sample Line Item Definitions

Most of the line item definitions can be modified by the bank to clarify individual bank reports, but there are certain exceptions, as noted.

Bank Assets
(Note: Include ONLY bank balances, NOT nonbank subsidiaries)

(1) *Federal Reserve Balance*

The sum of Federal Reserve due from bank balances.

(2) *Total Loans and Leases*

The sum of gross loans plus Other Real Estate Owned.

(3) *Free Securities*

This term is strictly limited to securities meeting the following characteristics: Salable securities held, securities available for pledging, unpledged securities in transit, and assets securitized. These securities are not encumbered in any way, and are of sufficient unit/transaction size and credit quality to be repurchased or sold in the market at will. Book value rather than market value is acceptable.

An accurate number for "Free Securities" is not typically available from the general ledger. Management's judgment is required to arrive at a representative figure in accordance with the definition provided. Various methods may be used, but should be subject to periodic testing to ensure reasonable accuracy.

(4) *Money Market Assets*

This term is limited strictly to the following instruments held externally in non-affiliated banks. No variance in the definition of "Money Market Assets" is allowed. Additional columns may be added, if necessary to provide an accurate portrayal of other liquid assets.

— Federal Funds Sold, both overnight and term (Do not include Repos)
— Negotiable CDs Purchased
— Foreign Deposits Placed, both overnight and term (Euro-dollar and other foreign currency)

Bank Liabilities
(Note: Include ONLY bank balances, NOT nonbank subsidiaries)

(5)   *DDA Net of Float*

Total demand deposit ledger balances, net of due from banks-deferred, due from Fed-deferred, and "other" cash items, such as items in process.

(6)   *Consumer Deposits*

Separate consumer accounts, which exceed $100M, if significant. The line (does not include DDA, which is reported separately) should reflect consumer deposits, such as:

— NOW accounts.
— Money market checking accounts.
— Non-transaction accounts, interest or noninterest bearing.
— CDs < $100M (net of public funds).
— Passbook savings.
— Money market savings.
— IRA and Keogh accounts.

(7)   *Federal Funds Purchased — Overnight*

The sum of Fed Funds Purchased as principal on an overnight basis.

(8)   *Fed Funds Purchased — Term*

The sum of Fed Funds Purchased as principal for a term longer than overnight.

(9)   *Foreign Deposits — Overnight*

All Eurodollars and foreign currency accepted as foreign branch liabilities on an overnight basis. Report retail deposits separate from wholesale or professional funds providers if significant.

(10)   *Foreign Deposits — Term*

All Eurodollars and foreign currency accepted as foreign branch deposits for a term longer than overnight. Report retail deposits separate from wholesale or professional funds providers, if significant.

(11)   *CDs >$100M*

Total balance of jumbo CDs (net of investment agreements and public funds). This category could include deposit notes, or other similar liabilities, if they are in excess of

$100M. Include the entire deposit if it is greater than $100M, but not deposits that are less than or equal to $100M if possible, based on MIS availability.

Note: For potential erosion estimates, it is best to assume that an entire deposit which exceeds $100M will leave the bank rather than the amount in excess of $100M. However, for identification of uninsured deposits for FDIC purposes, only the amount of each deposit exceeding $100M is technically uninsured.

(12)   *Other Sensitive Funds/Deposits*

Total of all funding sources that may exhibit unusual credit sensitivity that are not already defined.

(13)   *Treasury, Tax, and Loan*

The sum of the Treasury, Tax, and Loan balances.

(14)   *Fed Discount Window*

Total borrowings at the discount window.

Nonbank Assets (Parent)

(15)   *Short-Term Internal Investments*

Foreign deposits placed (from parent's perspective)

Other short-term liquid assets

Note: Typically, these parent company assets are placed in affiliated bank liability accounts, such as foreign deposits taken and therefore also are reflected on the bank's asset side — presumably in Money Market Assets. An understanding of how these funds flow from the parent to affiliate and back is critical in an analysis of the Funds Flow Analysis report to avoid double counting. It must be assumed that the bank's liabilities to the parent will have priority on the bank's liquid assets. Therefore, for analysis purposes they must be subtracted from the Money Market Asset number for an assessment of bank level liquidity.

122

(16)   *Short-Term __External__ Assets*

Cash, foreign deposits placed, other short-term liquid assets

Note: Ensure that these assets are not carried in the "consolidated" Funds Flow Analysis MMA figure (4). They represent liquid assets the parent maintains outside of its own corporation and are available to the parent over the listed total MMA figure in the Funds Flow Analysis Report.

Nonbank Liabilities (Parent)

(17)   *Commercial Paper, etc.*

Total commercial paper issued by the parent company or subsidiary, master notes, and any other short-term liability, including term debt or debt payments that are approaching maturity.

Appendix G
CONTINGENCY FUNDING PLAN SUMMARY
(Example format, tailor as appropriate)

POTENTIAL FUNDING EROSION

	CURRENT BALANCE	1 B/C	2 C	3 C/D	4 D	5 D/E
LARGE FUND PROVIDERS (from list)						
FED FUNDS						
CDs						
EURO TAKINGS / FOREIGN DEPOSITS						
COMMERCIAL PAPER						
SUB TOTAL						
OTHER UNINSURED FUND PROVIDERS						
FED FUNDS						
CDs						
EURO TAKINGS / FOREIGN DEPOSITS						
COMMERCIAL PAPER						
DDAs						
"CONSUMER" MMDA,						
SAVINGS,						
ETC.						

TOTAL UNINSURED FUNDS

INSURED FUNDS

TOTAL FUNDING BASE

OFF-BALANCE-SHEET FUNDING REQUIREMENTS

	CURRENT BALANCE	1 B/C	2 C	3 C/D	4 D	5 D/E
L/Cs						
LOAN COMMITMENTS						
SECURITIZATIONS (AMORTIZING)						
OPTIONS						
TOTAL OFF-BALANCE-SHEET ITEMS						

TOTAL POTENTIAL FUNDING EROSION

SOURCES OF FUNDS TO MEET DEMANDS
(WHICH MAY OR MAY NOT BE UTILIZED, DEPENDING ON NEED)
(ASSUMING NEEDED ASAP)

	IMMEDIATE	30 DAYS	60 DAYS	90 DAYS	180+ DAYS
SURPLUS MONEY MARKET ASSETS					
FREE SECURITIES					
ASSET SALES / SECURITIZATION					
CREDIT CARDS,					
AUTOs,					
CMOs,					
ETC.					
LOAN ATTRITION					
TOTAL INTERNAL SOURCES					

ESTIMATED LINE CAPACITY TO BORROW IN MARKET _____

BROKERED FUNDS CAPACITY _____

DISCOUNT WINDOW COLLATERAL "BORROWING VALUE" _____

Appendix H

Liquidity Information Requirements

(Note: The forms referred to in this list are included in the OCC MIS liquidity monitoring package. They are only samples or ideas. Tailor reports to fit your specific needs.

Daily Bank Information Needs

- Management should contact examiners immediately, if significant activity in the market or deterioration of any kind occurs throughout the day.

- Press articles, potentially damaging media, applicable Dow reports, and other pertinent information received over the wire — throughout the day.

- Wire room activity report — daily and periodically as appropriate.

- Daylight OD numbers.

- Stock quote.

- CD rate survey.

- Funds flow analysis (see form).

- Fed funds summary (see form).

- Net intercompany funding positions report (see form).

- Total deposit trends report (see form).

- Damage assessment report (see form).

- Summary balance sheets on all banks and affiliates.

- Sources and uses analysis (see form).

- Meet with examiners to discuss reports.

- Close of business estimates (see form).

Daily Examiner Requirements

- Management should contact examiners immediately, if significant activity in the market or deterioration of any kind occurs throughout the day.

- Press articles, potentially damaging media, applicable Dow reports, and other pertinent information received over the wire — throughout the day. +

- Wire room activity report — daily and periodically, as appropriate. **

- Daylight OD numbers.

- Stock quote.

- CD rate survey. #

- Funds flow analysis (see form). +

- Fed funds summary (see form). +

- Net intercompany funding positions report (see form). **, +

- Total deposit trends (see form). +

- Damage assessment reports (see form). **, +

- Summary balance sheets on all banks and affiliates. **

- Meet with management to discuss reports. **

- Prepare daily e-mail. +

- Sources and uses analysis (see form).

- Narrative of (1) sources and uses analysis and (2) any important events.

- Close of business estimates.

Monthly until conditions exist that adversely threaten the company's funding position.

** Needed only when bank is under examination or conditions exist that would affect the company's funding position adversely.

+ To be faxed to District and Washington analysts.

Weekly Examiner Requirements

	When Available	Responsibility

- Unfunded commitment report **

- Maturities report

- Consolidated maturities summary +

- Summary lead banks balance sheets with significant changes explained **

- Due from/to correspondent bank summary **

- Trust balance (secured portion) **

- ALCO packet

- Fed discount window collateral (see form) +

- TT&L collateral (see form) +

- Attend bank ALCO **

- Loan sales report (may be in ALCO Packet)

- Parent company weekly cash flow +

- Top 20 customer analysis (consolidated)

- Jumbo CD rates comparisons +

	When Available	Responsibility
• Foreign funding customer listing		
• Liquidity enhancement programs (see form) +		
• Commercial paper maturities +		

** Needed only when bank is under examination or conditions exist that would affect the company's funding position adversely.

+ To be faxed to District and Washington analysts.

Monthly Examiner Requirements

	When Available	Responsibility
• Detailed month-end balance sheets on all banks **		
• Euro takings		
• Consolidated balance sheet **, +		
• Bank rating agency reports (or as change occurs) +		
• Contingency plan **		
• Uninsured/uncollateralized deposits**,+		
• Total trust deposits at risk **		
• ALCO packet (corporate) **		
• Attend corporate ALCO **		
• External funding lines report (see form) +		

** Needed only when bank is under examination or conditions exist that would affect the company's funding position adversely.

+ To be faxed or overnight mailed to District and Washington analysts.

Appendix I

Capital Call Meeting Agenda

Purpose Of Meeting:

- Inform board of the findings of the examination currently underway at the bank, particularly with respect to the bank's capital support.

- Find out status of plans or efforts to obtain additional capital.

- Describe what will occur subsequent to the meeting.

- Answer any questions the board may have.

Opening Discussion:

- As a result of losses identified during the exam, the bank is critically undercapitalized. If the exam were to conclude today, the bank would be closed and placed into receivership.

- Although the exam is coming to a close, the OCC is open to any viable and realistic plan that will restore adequate capital support. We can stop the process at any time up to the actual moment that the bank is placed into receivership. We do not want to close a bank if we can avoid it. Therefore, as things develop, the bank must keep examiners well informed.

- Discuss what is meant by a viable and realistic capital plan, noting the difference between actions to effect the recapitalization and expressions of interest.

- The losses and ALLL analysis has been reviewed by a team of senior examiners to ensure that the ALLL and losses have been classified properly consistent with the OCC's policies and procedures.

Exam Review: The EIC highlights briefly the scope of the exam and any other significant items.

Capital Analysis: Analyst distributes and discusses capital analysis sheet.

Ask board if they have questions / update us on capital plans

FDIC Preparation Process and Access Resolution:

- Must begin to prepare early as shared goal is to have failure be as least disruptive as possible.

- Discuss the following: informational package, informational bid meeting, variety of dispositions, whole bank/TAPA bidders need more information, therefore, need for access resolution.

- Describe access resolution process, options and general time frames.

- Distribute access resolution and get it executed.

Closing Items:
- Note the sensitivity of the information discussed. Rumors and speculation in the local community could cause a liquidity crisis, therefore, the bank should plan for and monitor changes in liquidity.

- Discuss options regarding uninsured deposits.

- Discuss options regarding legal lending limits. Ensure that exam findings are reflected in Call Reports. Note that although time is short, the OCC is receptive to a realistic and viable plan. Respond to any questions.

SUMMARY OF CRITICIZED ASSETS

	OAEM	SUBSTANDARD	DOUBTFUL	LOSS
Loans	0	0	0	0
OREO	0	0	0	0
Other Assets	0	0	0	0
Accrued Interest	0	0	0	0
TOTAL	0	0	0	0

ALLOWANCE FOR LOAN AND LEASE LOSSES (ALLL)

Based upon a review of the loan portfolio and after considering losses charged off at this examination, an adequate ALLL balance equals $.

CAPITAL ANALYSIS USING INFORMATION AS OF *(date)*

ALLOWANCE FOR LOAN AND LEASE LOSSES (ALLL)

0	BALANCE ON
0	*less* EXAMINATION LOAN LOSSES
0	BALANCE AFTER LOAN LOSSES
0	*plus* PROVISION EXPENSE NEEDED TO RESTORE ALLL ADEQUACY
0	ENDING ALLL BALANCE

TANGIBLE EQUITY CAPITAL (As defined in 12 CFR 6.2)

0	BALANCE ON
0	*less* LOSSES CHARGED TO RETAINED EARNINGS
0	BALANCE AFTER LOSSES
0	*less* PROVISION EXPENSE NEEDED TO RESTORE ALLL ADEQUACY
0	ENDING TANGIBLE EQUITY CAPITAL BALANCE
0	TOTAL ASSETS ON

0.00%	ENDING TANGIBLE EQUITY CAPITAL RATIO

EQUITY CAPITAL NEEDED TO RESTORE MINIMUM ADEQUATE CAPITAL SUPPORT

0	TOTAL ASSETS ON
X 5%	MINIMUM PERCENT OF ASSETS NEEDED AS EQUITY CAPITAL
0	MINIMUM REQUIRED EQUITY CAPITAL BALANCE
0	*less* ENDING TANGIBLE EQUITY CAPITAL BALANCE

$1.2 MILLION	REQUIRED CAPITAL INJECTION TO RESTORE MINIMUM ADEQUATE CAPITAL

THIS AMOUNT REPRESENTS THE EQUITY CAPITAL INJECTION NECESSARY TO ACHIEVE MINIMUM CAPITAL ADEQUACY AT THIS TIME. THIS AMOUNT MAY NOT REPRESENT THE TOTAL INJECTION THAT WOULD BE SUFFICIENT TO ENSURE LONG-TERM VIABILITY OF THE BANK. ADDITIONAL CAPITAL INJECTIONS MAY BE NECESSARY.

Appendix J

Resolution Worksheet and EIC Information Questionnaire

(The SPSF analyst will complete this first page.)

Resolution Worksheet for Law Department — Provided by SPSF to BAS and LIT for use in preparation of bank closing documents (including the Declaration of SPSF Director).

Bank Name:
Bank Address:

Charter No.:

SPSF Examiner:

Time and Date Documents Required:

Time and Date of Pre-Closing Meeting: N/A

Time and Date of Pre-Closing Briefing with Senior Deputy Comptroller: N/A

Time and Date of Closing:

Closing Documents to be Signed by:
    Name: Leann G. Britton
    Title: Senior Deputy Comptroller for Bank Supervision Operations

OCC District Office: Central

PCA Notification letters:

	LETTER SENT	CRP DUE	CRP APPROVED OR DISAPPROVED
UNDERCAPITALIZED			
SIGNIFICANTLY UNDERCAPITALIZED			
CRITICALLY UNDERCAPITALIZED			

The following is information to be acquired once you know the bank you are examining will become critically undercapitalized pursuant to prompt corrective action ("PCA") (tangible equity ratio of 2.0 percent or less, <u>see</u> 12 CFR 6.4(b)(5)), or will otherwise meet the criteria for appointment of the FDIC as receiver (<u>see</u> 12 USC 191 and 12 USC 1821(c)(5)). This information, much of which is outside the scope of a normal examination, will be needed by the SPSF analyst to complete preparations for appointing the FDIC receiver for the bank.

Since PCA requires the OCC take action against critically undercapitalized banks within 90 days, please fax or E-mail the completed questionnaire to SPSF as quickly as possible. The SPSF fax number is 202-874-5214.

In some instances, certain information may be difficult or time consuming to obtain. If so, please contact the assigned SPSF analyst at 202-874-4450 to determine if significant resources should be expended. In almost every case it will be better to send in a partially completed questionnaire than to hold it for two weeks while completing one or two missing items. The SPSF analyst generally will need this information to prepare for holding the capital call meeting.

1. Please provide the name, address, phone number (include an after hours phone number if applicable), fax number, and days/hours (lobby and drive-up), as applicable, for the main office and each of the bank's other locations (including stand alone bank ATM's):

2. Charter number and date of charter:

3. Does the bank have trust powers?
   If so, are they active?

4. Date of examination:
   Date the exam commenced:

5. In brief paragraphs, summarize when and why the bank initially became a problem (4 or 5 rated) and deteriorated to the point of becoming critically undercapitalized. Also, in your opinion, what are the primary causes of the bank's deterioration and likely failure? (Always highlight any special problems, such as lending concentrations, poor underwriting standards, fraud, or insider abuse.)

6.   Insider abuse?

7.   Fraud?
      Briefly describe any fraudulent activity found in the bank. Was there any loss to the bank?
      If so, is it significant in the failure? Did the bank make any criminal referrals?

8.   History of enforcement actions? (Types, dates, and record of compliance):

9.   CMPs referrals, criminal referrals, or removal actions or recommendations?

      a)   At prior exams: Dates? Status?
      b)   At this exam: (describe reasons, amount, status)

10.   Classifications at current examination (note if preliminary):

	Loans	Other Assets	Total
SM			
SUBSTANDARD			
DOUBTFUL			
LOSS			

11.   Capital Call Meeting Recap (date, location, and information as of   ):

      Date and Location:

      (information as of   )
      Beginning tangible equity:
      Beginning total assets:

      OCC directed provision expense:
      OCC directed OREO charge off:
      Other OCC directed charges to earnings:
      Resulting tangible equity:
      Resulting total assets:
      Resulting tangible equity ratio:

Required capital injection:

12. Financial information:

	Last Call (date)	Exam Date (date)	Most Recent Month-End (date)
Total Assets			
Total Deposits			
ALLL			
Tier 1 capital			
PMSRs in Tier 1			
PCCRs in Tier 1			
Tier 2 capital			
Cumulative perpetual preferred stock			
Tangible equity ratio:			
YTD Net Income:			

13. Bank principal shareholders percentage of ownership

     a) Name, number of shares, and percentage of total shares

Shareholder	# of shares owned	% of outstanding

     b) Is there a voting trust agreement? If so, who controls it?

     c) How much of the stock does the current board presently own?

14. If owned by a holding company, provide names and percentage of ownership for all who own more than 5 percent of the holding company.

     a) Name, number of shares, and percentage of total shares
     b) How much of the stock does the current board presently own?

15. Deposits:

    a)   Amount of uninsured deposits? How many customers? Primarily business or personal?

    b)   Any public funds? How much uninsured?

    c)   Amount of brokered deposits? (use FDIC definition). How much matures in more than one year? Any concentrations?

16. Contingent Liabilities:

17. Standards for appointment of the FDIC as receiver. Identify <u>and provide support</u> for each of the following that apply. (See 12 USC 191 and 1821(c)(5). Also, consult with SPSF analyst.):

    ___ a)   The bank's assets are less than its obligations to its creditors.

    ___ b)   There has been substantial dissipation of assets or earnings due to
         ___ (i)   violation of statute or regulation (list cites and explain violations), or
         ___ (ii)   unsafe or unsound practice (describe the practice).

    ___ c)   The bank is in an unsafe or unsound condition to transact business (describe the condition).

    ___ d)   There is willful violation of a final order to cease and desist (cite article of the order, explain the violation, and give evidence of the willfulness).

    ___ e)   There is
         ___ (i)   concealment of the bank's books, papers, records or assets (give details), or
         ___ (ii)   refusal to submit the bank's books, papers, records, or affairs for inspection to any examiner, or to any lawful agent of the OCC (give details).

    ___ f)   The bank is likely to be unable to pay its obligations or meet its depositors' demands in the normal course of business (describe the liquidity situation).

    ___ g)   The bank has incurred or is likely to incur losses that will deplete all or substantially all of its capital, and there is no reasonable prospect for the bank to become adequately capitalized without federal assistance.

_   h)   There is a:

    _   Violation of law or regulation (give cite), or

    _   Unsafe or unsound practice or condition (describe) that is likely to cause

      —   insolvency, or

      —   substantial dissipation of assets or earnings (give details);

      —   weaken the bank's condition (give details);

      —   otherwise seriously prejudice the interests of the bank's depositors or the deposit insurance fund (give details).

_   i)   The bank, by resolution of its board of directors or its shareholders, consents to the appointment (give date of board or shareholders meeting).

_   j)   The bank ceases to be an insured institution (describe how and when that occurred or is expected to occur).

_   k)   The bank is undercapitalized and

    _   has no reasonable prospects of becoming adequately capitalized;

    _   fails to become adequately capitalized when required to do so (provide dates when the bank was so required);

    _   fails to submit an acceptable capital restoration plan to the OCC within the time prescribed (provide date when CRP was due) or;

    _   materially fails to implement a capital restoration plan (provide details of material failings).

_   l)   The bank is critically undercapitalized, or otherwise has substantially insufficient capital.

_   m)   The bank's board of directors has fewer than five members (provide details and relevant dates).

18.   Liquidity: *(Provide these items upon specific request of the Washington SPSF analyst, if liquidity is or may become critical, or if you checked item 14(f) as a reason for appointment of the FDIC as receiver.)

    a)   FRB line: How much? Type and amount of collateral pledged?

    b)   Correspondent lines of credit: Who? Secured or unsecured? Amount? Collateral?

    c)   How much in fed funds sold?

    d)   Are there any unpledged securities?

    e)   What is the due from banks time?

138

f)　What are the average working cash balances?

g)　How much cash is withdrawn from the bank weekly?

h)　What is the bank's average daily cash letter?

19.　Type of market bank is located in (*e.g.,* diverse, agricultural, etc.)

20.　Full names and titles of executive officers:

COB:
CEO:
President:
SVP and Senior Lender:
CFO:

21.　Local Federal Reserve Bank?

22.　Capital:

a)　Authorized but unissued shares of stock?
b)　Par value of stock?
c)　Pre-emptive rights?

23.　Did the bank receive CPA audits while under SPSF?

a)　Years and by whom?
b)　Opinions rendered?
c)　Did the audits disclose any of the bank's problems?

24.　Telephone and fax numbers of local media.

a)　Newspapers.
b)　Major radio stations.
c)　Television stations.

25.　OCC EIC:

a)　Full name:
b)　Home telephone:
c)　Telephone number where EIC can be reached if not at bank:
d)　Duty Station phone and Fax number:
e)　ADC name and phone number:

26. Are there any regulators in the bank in the EIC's absence?

27. Hotel near the bank (Provide only if requested by Washington analyst).

28. Litigation, by or against the bank. Explain.

29. Fidelity (blanket) bond — amount, expiration date, any claims.

30. Directors and officers (D&O) insurance — amount, for whom, expiration date, any claims.

31. Management contracts, severance pay provisions (if any).

Appendix K

Bank Failure Questionnaire

<u>Overview</u>

Examiners in charge of failed banks complete this questionnaire and record their subjective assessments as to why the bank failed. Data collected from the questionnaires is entered into a database maintained in the SPSF Division in Washington. This information is used to draw conclusions regarding failure trends and to provide a database on historical examination activity. For more information, contact the SPSF Division at 202-874-4450.

<u>Instructions</u>

Worksheet I contains judgmental information about the bank. There are two distinct rating criteria. Numerical ratings assigned to the heading of each section **(e.g., Policy, Planning, and Management Quality; Audits, Controls, and Systems)** are used to indicate the extent that the particular area was a <u>factor in the deterioration and failure</u> of the bank.

Numerical ratings assigned to the characteristics under the headings (all other data elements in Worksheet I) are used to indicate the extent that the condition <u>existed</u> in the problem bank. The ratings for the headings (contribution to failure) and the characteristics (existing in the problem bank) will not necessarily be the same.

A scale of "0" to "5" should be used to rate each element, "0" indicating "no contribution or condition" and "5" indicating "very much a contribution or condition." If insufficient information is available to determine a rating, assign a "9." If information was available, but you do not feel comfortable in assigning a rating, enter a "7."

Worksheet II contains factual information about the bank. This may be filled out by the SPSF analyst or EIC. Please provide examination data in reverse chronological order, beginning with the ratings assigned at the exam during which the bank failed at the top. Ideally, CAMELS should be listed as far back as possible. <u>Exclude off-sites.</u> Please note that exam dates and CAMELS ratings may be accessed through the Stat Data Function on NBSVDS, however you may need to go to ROEs to determine whether activity was an off-site or on-site exam.

<u>One questionnaire should be completed for each failed bank. However, in the case of failed multibank holding companies, it may be more appropriate to complete only one questionnaire for the lead bank.</u>

WORKSHEET I: Significant Characteristics and Conditions of Problem Banks Primary Causes of Bank Failure

Bank Name: _____

Charter # _____

POLICY, PLANNING, AND MANAGEMENT QUALITY: ___

Board Lacks Necessary Banking Knowledge: ___
Board Uninformed of Bank's Operations or Passive Board: ___
Overly Aggressive Board: (excessively growth minded/liberal in credit views): ___
No or Poor Operating and Strategic Planning:
Decision-making Process Lacks Adequate MIS: ___
Poor Judgment in Decision-making (not insider abuse or fraud): ___
Decisions Made by Dominant Individual (CEO, COB): ___
Management Behavior Negatively Affected by Affiliate Influence: ___
CEO Lacks Experience or Capability: ___
CEO of Poor Integrity: ___
Mgmt Team Lacks Diversity and Depth of Experience
    (qualitative assessment of background, etc.): ___
Inexperienced/Inadequate Mgmt/Officers/Staff, other than CEO
    (quantitative, #, tenure, turnover): ___
Inadequate Controls or Supervision of Key Officers or Departments: ___
Inadequate or Failed to Follow Policies:
    Loan: ___
    Investment: ___
    A/L Management: ___
    Concentrations: ___
    Conflict of Interest: ___

AUDITS, CONTROLS, AND SYSTEMS: ___

Inadequate Controls/Systems to Ensure Compliance
    with Policies and Law: ___
Inadequate Internal Audit System: ___
Inadequate Problem Loan Identification System: ___

ASSET QUALITY: —

Loans:
    Excessive Financial Statement Exceptions: —
    Poor Collateral Documentation/Perfection: —
    Liberal Terms/Failure to Enforce Repayment
        (Inadequate collection/capitalized interest):   —
    Excessive Loan Growth in Relation to Management or Staff
        Abilities, Controls and Systems, Funding Sources, etc.:   —
    Out-of-Area Lending: —
    Overlending: High Loan to Debt Service Ability: —
    Collateral-based Lending or Insufficient Cash Flow Analysis: —
    Inadequate Participations Purchased Guidelines: —
    Unwarranted Concentrations of Credit: —
    Substantial Loan Quality Deterioration Attributed to Causes Beyond
      the Bank□s Control in
        Agriculture: —
        Oil and Gas: —
        Real Estate:
Investments:
    Poor Risk Selection in Purchases: —
    Improper Maturity Selection: —

LIQUIDITY/FUNDS MANAGEMENT: —

    Failure to Develop Sufficient Core Deposits: —
    Mismatched A/L Maturities (rate risk):   —
    Reliance on Volatile Liabilities
        (>$100M, Not Necessarily Brokered):   —
    Premium Paid (relative to peer) for Funds: —
    Inadequate Liquid Assets or Secondary Sources of Liquidity: —

NON FUNDING EXPENSES: —

    Significant Litigation: Legal Expense or Judgment: —
    Excessive Fixed Asset Expense (occupancy):   —
    Trading or Investment Speculation Losses (through normal operations):   —
    High Debt Service or Dividend Payout (to finance acquisitions, etc.):   —
    Abnormal Salaries, Remuneration or Management Fees: —

EARNINGS:

    High Loss Provision Expense: —

    High Nonaccrual or Nonperforming Assets: —

    Below "Target" NIM (primarily pricing errors, not results of

        poor credit judgment as in loan elements):   —

    High Non-Funding Expense: —

INSIDER ABUSE: —

    Negative Management Influence by Directors, Officers, or

        Shareholders: —

    Self-dealing: —

    Board or Shareholder Dependence on Bank for

        Income or Services (individually):   —

    Inappropriate Transactions with Affiliates: —

    Unauthorized Transactions by Management Officials: —

FRAUD: —

    Material Fraud Attributed to:

        COB: —

        Board Member: —

        CEO: —

        Other Management Official:

        Principal Shareholder: —

        Outsider: —

ENVIRONMENT/ECONOMY: —

    Poor Physical Location: —

    Depressed Economic Sector

        Agriculture: —

        Oil and Gas: —

        RE: —

        Other (specify): _____   —

    Major Employer Failed or Left the Area: —

    Local Catastrophe (specify): _____   —

WORKSHEET II: Supplemental Information

BANK NAME: _____

CHARTER #: _____

STATE: (two letter post office code) _____

DATE OF CHARTER: _____

DATE OF FAILURE: _____

ADMINISTRATIVE ACTION: (enter completed or effective date)

MOU

FA _____ _____

C&D _____ _____

Other

EXAMINATION DATA: (Reverse Chronological Order)

Exam as of Date	**C**	**A**	**M**	**E**	**L**	**S** /	**C**	Compliance with Document C / NC
_____	__	__	__	__	__	__	__	__
_____	__	__	__	__	__	__	__	__
_____	__	__	__	__	__	__	__	__
_____	__	__	__	__	__	__	__	__
_____	__	__	__	__	__	__	__	__
_____	__	__	__	__	__	__	__	__
_____	__	__	__	__	__	__	__	__
_____	__	__	__	__	__	__	__	__
_____	__	__	__	__	__	__	__	__

AVG ASSET SIZE:

    __ LESS THAN $ 15MM
    __ $ 15MM TO $ 30MM
    __ $ 30MM TO $ 50MM
    __ $ 50MM TO $100MM
    __ $100MM TO $1B
    __ OVER $1B

RECAPITALIZATION EFFORTS: __ NONE   __ FAILED

$____ AMT	____ DATE	____ SOURCE
$____ AMT	____ DATE	____ SOURCE
$____ AMT	____ DATE	____ SOURCE
$____ AMT	____ DATE	____ SOURCE
$____ AMT	____ DATE	____ SOURCE

SOURCE CODES: HC - Holding Company
                            PU - Public Offering
                            PI - Private Offering
                            PO - Private Outsider

MARKET CHARACTERISTICS:

POPULATION:
    Major metropolitan 250M plus   _____
    Metropolitan area 50M to 250M   _____
    Urban area 5M to 50M   _____
    Rural area less than 5M   _____

ECONOMIC BASE:
    Diversified   _____
    Single Industry   _____
        Agriculture   _____
        Oil and Gas   _____
        Real Estate   _____
    Single Employer   _____

TARGETED MARKET:
    Specialized   _____
    Full Service   _____

BANK OWNERSHIP AND CONTROL:

ACQUIRED BY CONTROL GROUP	DATE	TYPE
	_____	_____
	_____	_____
	_____	_____
	_____	_____
	_____	_____

Control Group Codes: SG - Small Group
PH - Publicly Held
CB - Chain Bank
HC - Multibank Holding Company
HO - One Bank Holding Company

NATURE OF OWNERSHIP AT THE TIME COMPOSITE 5 RATING ASSIGNED:

Publicly Held   _____
Closely Held   _____
One Bank HC - Public   _____
One Bank HC - Private   _____
Multibank HC*   _____
Chain Banking Group*   _____

SIGNIFICANT CHANGE IN MANAGEMENT:
(Enter Date)

COB:	____	____	____	____
CEO:	____	____	____	____
COB/CEO:	____	____	____	____
SLO:	____	____	____	____
OTHER SENIOR OFFICERS:	____	____	____	____

* If Multibank Holding Company or Chain Bank, Total Number of Related National Banks that failed _____

Appendix L

Closing Book
Table of Contents

NAME OF BANK
CITY, STATE   CHARTER #

(A)   Bank Closing Check List

(B)   Telephone List

(C)   Capital Call Worksheet

(D)   Charge Off Letter

(E)   Fact Sheet and Legal Worksheet
           EIC Information Gathering Questionnaire

(F)   CUB Notification Letter
           Letter of Authorization of OCC Personnel
           Letter to FDIC Re: Assistance in Closing
           Letter to FRB Re: Emergency Approval Process

(G)   Declaration

(H)   Decision of the Comptroller of the Currency

(I)   News Release

(J)   Memo to Senior Deputy Comptroller for Economic Analysis and Public Affairs

(K)   Comptroller's Appointment of Receiver
           Comptroller's Letter Appointing FDIC as Receiver

(L)   Comptroller's Letter to CEO Advising of Closure
           Comptroller's Letter to the Deputy Comptroller

(M)   FAX to FRB and Board of Governors

(Mc)   Memo to OCC Divisions Advising of Appointment of FDIC as Receiver

(N)   FDIC Acknowledgment of Receipt of ROEs

(O)   Media Coverage

(P)   Failed Bank Analysis and Statistical Data Sheets

(Q)   BPR

(R)   Stock Subscription Agreement

(S)   FDIC Board Resolution Case
                FDIC Acceptance of Appointment as Receiver

Appendix M

Sample Closure Script for SDC, Decision Maker

Name of Bank, City, State

EIC: _____   SPSF:_____

(To be prepared by SPSF)

Is the lobby cleared and has the bank completed its business day?

Please provide me with some facts:

1.   What is the bank's present tangible equity? $_____

2.   What is the bank's present total assets? $_____

3.   What is the bank's present tangible equity ratio?_____%

4.   In your opinion, has the bank incurred or is it likely to incur losses that will deplete all or substantially all of its capital, and is there no reasonable prospect for the bank to become adequately capitalized without federal assistance?

5.   In your opinion, is the bank undercapitalized, did it fail to become adequately capitalized when required to do so, and did it fail to submit an acceptable capital restoration plan to the OCC?

6.   Is the bank critically undercapitalized?

7.   Does the bank's board of directors have fewer than five members?

I hereby appoint the FDIC receiver for the bank. Please deliver the appropriate closing papers to the bank and the FDIC.

Appendix N

OCC Closing Manager Procedures

Day of Closing

1. Hold briefing for OCC personnel who will assist you in the closing of branches of uninsured banks [or satellite offices of federal branches and agencies]. Distribute:

    - Copy of Comptroller's appointment of receiver.
    - Copy of news release.
    - Copy of out of order signs.
    - Copy of closing speech, if prepared.

    Discuss their need to call you once they are at branch site, and any contingency actions which might be needed.

2. Go to bank/federal branch with EIC.

3. Meet president [or, in case of federal branch, the general manager]. Discuss:

    - Likelihood of closure.
    - Ask for copy of most recent daily statement.
    - Any large losses or adjustments since the last exam.
    - Need for place to work, telephone with at least two outside lines.
    - President should tell bank branch personnel to expect OCC personnel.
    - Ask president to remain on-site if possible in case we need help.

4. Secure work space.

5. Calculate script numbers:

    - Date of final exam.
    - All numbers from finalized exam, plus any significant interim asset losses taken.
    - Equity from most recent daily statement.
    - Provision expense from exam if not already taken (taken straight from equity).
    - OREO, non-accrual losses (taken straight from equity) if not already taken.
    - If liquidity failure, get liquidity and cash letter numbers.

6. Call SPSF backup.

    - Give direct phone number, extension and fax number.

- Give script numbers.

7. Locate receiver, if he or she did not accompany you to the bank.

    - Alert receiver to the need to secure electronic and physical data and computer access.

    - Alert receiver to the need to evaluate and address pending capital markets transactions.

8. About three hours before projected closing, you and EIC meet with president. Discuss:

    - Any possibility of event to delay insolvency or liquidity crisis.
    - Closing procedures and what will occur.
    - Need to have drive through and lobby cleared of customers at closing time.
    - Vault must stay open after closing for cash count by receiver's staff.
    - Employee salaries and accrued vacation should be cut through the end of today. No unusual entries, such as bonuses. If payroll servicer cannot issue checks today, bank will have to issue cashier's checks to all employees to be cashed before closing.
    - Determine if bank has filed any claims with bond carrier.
    - Request ROEs, enforcement documents, and OCC correspondence.
    - Locate original charter [license], and trust powers.
    - "Business as usual" to inquiries.

9. Work on:

    - Failed bank questionnaire with EIC.
    - Receiver's acknowledgment of ROEs.
    - Make OCC assignments to cover branch phones, EIC phone, drive-through, lobby postings, and vault.
    - Get calls from OCC branch personnel to receive their phone number and to give them extension to call just before closing.

10. About one hour to 30 minutes before closing meet again with president. Explain:

    - Need to notify employees of meeting shortly after projected closing time. President may want to say a few words to staff, at that time.
    - Need help in shutting down drive-throughs, clearing lobby.
    - Ensure ATM servicer posts electronic notice on network that bank is closed and ATMs are unavailable.

11. Meet with receiver:

    - Give ROEs and correspondence.
    - Get ROE acknowledgment signed by receiver, give him/her a copy.

12. Clear and close drive-throughs, night depository, and ATMs.

13. If necessary, assign OCC employee to vault to ensure it remains open.

14. Clear lobby.

15. Receive call from Washington, converse with Senior Deputy Comptroller (SDC), until all facilities are secure.

16. Receive calls from OCC branch personnel; ensure those facilities are secured. Ask that they remain on the phone, until the bank is closed by SDC.

17. EIC goes through script with SDC; bank declared closed.

18. Tell OCC branch personnel bank is closed.

19. Hand receivership papers to receiver:

- Appointment of receiver.
- Letter of appointment of receiver.
- Receiver's acceptance of appointment.
- Copy of news release.

20. Give president:

- Appointment of receiver.
- Letter to CEO [and parent bank].
- Copy of news release.

21. Have OCC personnel post all pages of appointment of receiver and news release on outside of all public entrances.

22. Address bank employees:

- Introduce yourself. Explain that the OCC, which regulates this bank, has just made the decision to close the bank because (give reasons). Introduce receiver and state s/he will answer your questions. Allow president to say a few words.
- Stay while receiver introduces and goes over initial procedures.

23. Take charter [license] and leave.

OCC Closing Manager Procedures

After Closing

1. Complete closing book and give it to SPSF secretary for filing. Include:

   - Signed decision and appointment of receiver.
   - Faxes to FRB, FRS, District Office [parent bank, home country supervisor].
   - News release.
   - Copy of failed bank questionnaire.
   - Any media coverage, collected by EIC.
   - Receiver's acknowledgment of receivership.
   - Receiver's signed receipt of ROEs.

2. Forward Failed Bank Questionnaire to SPSF analyst for input into data base.

3. Send original charter, [license], trust powers to Central Records. Send National Filing System bank files (cleaned out of extraneous material) back to District Office.

4. SMS entries:

   - OSE or analysis, briefly stating date, reason for failure, placement into receivership.
   - Delegate bank/branch back to district and unassign Washington and supervisory office analyst.
   - Terminate enforcement action(s), if any, with "failure" as reason.

5. Notify district that analysis was entered in SMS, bank/branch delegated back, and someone in Licensing should inactivate institution.

6. Notify SPSF secretary, so s/he can prepare memo to OCC divisions:

   - Bank/branch name, charter/license number, and location.
   - Failure date.
   - Name of receiver.

Branch Closing Procedures for OCC Personnel

[For branches of uninsured national bank and satellite offices of federal branches and agencies]

Your functions at the branch will be to:

- Monitor liquidity and branch activity.
- Make sure the lobby closes promptly at the designated closing time and that drive-through windows and ATMs are closed simultaneously.
- Make sure that the vault, safe, etc. and all records remain accessible for the receiver and his or her staff.
- Preliminarily locate branch charter and remove upon closing.
- Speak to bank employees after closing and introduce receiver's staff.

Please arrive at branch office at _____. Meet with the branch manager and inform her or him that you are there to monitor the activity of the branch. The manager will have received a call from the president [general manager] to expect you and to cooperate. After meeting with the manager, please notify us at the main office number _____.

During the day, monitor liquidity and observe branch activity while maintaining a low profile. Immediately call the main office if there is any unusual activity. Determine whether the branch has a night depository, drive-through, or ATMs. Locate the branch certificate issued by the OCC. You will be joined by a member of the receiver's staff shortly before the closing.

Approximately 30 minutes before the closing time, inform the branch manager that there is a likelihood that the bank will be closed today by the OCC. Ask the manager to remain available until closing time. Enlist his or her cooperation in shutting down the drive-through after closing and expediting the departure of after-hour customers.

Ask the manager to promptly close the branch lobby and drive-through windows at _____. You should allow any customer in the branch to complete their business. Drive-through traffic at the window should be serviced. However, any additional traffic in line should not be serviced. After the present transaction is completed, the window should be closed via a sign or shade. Also secure the night depository (lock it and place Out of Service sign on it) and shut down the ATM (turn off and put up Out of Order sign). No relatives, spouses, or friends should be in the branch after closing. This includes the press. The manager should be instructed accordingly.

Once the lobbies and drive-throughs are cleared at all the banking offices, the Senior Deputy Comptroller will discuss the bank's condition with the EIC. If satisfied that the bank is to be placed into receivership, he or she will declare it thus. When this occurs, you will be notified from the main office by an OCC examiner. You should then post all pages of the Appointment of Receiver and News Release on outside of all public entrances. Make an announcement to bank employees, telling them what has occurred and that the receiver's staff will meet with them. The branch manager may want to make a short comment, prior to comments by the receiver's staff.

Avoid any discussion on the future of bank employees. Be particularly sensitive to employees feelings under these stressful circumstances.

Once the process is completed, and the receiver is in control, you should leave the branch with the branch certificate. Prior to leaving, please notify us at the main office. If the press is present, do not offer any comment; just state "no comment" and walk to your car. Do not identify yourself. If pressed for a comment, refer them to the posted News Release and state that they can call the OCC Communications Division in Washington at (202) 874-4700.